QUEEN OF SHEBA

◆ ◆ ◆

❖ ANCIENT WORLD LEADERS ❖

✦ ANCIENT WORLD LEADERS ✦

QUEEN OF SHEBA

NAOMI LUCKS

CHELSEA HOUSE
PUBLISHERS
An imprint of Infobase Publishing

Frontispiece: Queen of Sheba. Painting by Jean Jules Badin, circa 1870.

Chelsea House
An imprint of Infobase Publishing
132 West 31st Street
New York, NY 10001

Library of Congress Cataloging-in-Publication Data

Lucks, Naomi.
  Queen of Sheba / Naomi Lucks.
    p. cm. — (Ancient world leaders)
  Includes bibliographical references and index.
  ISBN 978-0-7910-9579-9 (hardcover)
  1. Sheba, Queen of. 2. Sheba, Queen of—Legends. 3. Queens—Yemen (Repubic)—Biography.
4. Sabaeans—Kings and rulers—Biography. I. Title. II. Series.

  DS247.Y47S545 2008
  939'.4902092—dc22   2008004872
  [B]

Chelsea House books are available at special discounts when purchased in bulk quantities for businesses, associations, institutions, or sales promotions. Please call our Special Sales Department in New York at (212) 967-8800 or (800) 322-8755.

You can find Chelsea House on the World Wide Web at http://www.chelseahouse.com

Text design by Lina Farinella
Cover design by Jooyoung An

Printed in United States of America

Bang NMSG 10 9 8 7 6 5 4 3 2 1

This book is printed on acid-free paper.

All links and Web addresses were checked and verified to be correct at the time of publication. Because of the dynamic nature of the Web, some addresses and links may have changed since publication and may no longer be valid.

CONTENTS

Arthur M. Schlesinger, Jr.
On Leadership

L eadership, it may be said, is really what makes the world go round. Love no doubt smoothes the passage; but love is a private transaction between consenting adults. Leadership is a public transaction with history. The idea of leadership affirms the capacity of individuals to move, inspire, and mobilize masses of people so that they act together in pursuit of an end. Sometimes leadership serves good purposes, sometimes bad; but whether the end is benign or evil, great leaders are those men and women who leave their personal stamp on history.

Now, the very concept of leadership implies the proposition that individuals can make a difference. This proposition has never been universally accepted. From classical times to the present day, eminent thinkers have regarded individuals as no more than the agents and pawns of larger forces, whether the gods and goddesses of the ancient world or, in the modern era, race, class, nation, the dialectic, the will of the people, the spirit of the times, history itself. Against such forces, the individual dwindles into insignificance.

So contends the thesis of historical determinism. Tolstoy's great novel *War and Peace* offers a famous statement of the case. Why, Tolstoy asked, did millions of men in the Napoleonic Wars, denying their human feelings and their common sense, move back and forth across Europe slaughtering their fellows? "The war," Tolstoy answered, "was bound to happen simply because it was bound to happen." All prior history determined it. As for leaders, they, Tolstoy said, "are but the labels that serve to give a name to an end and, like labels, they have the least possible connection with the event." The greater the leader, "the more conspicuous the inevitability and the predestination of every act he commits." The leader, said Tolstoy, is "the slave of history."

Determinism takes many forms. Marxism is the determinism of class. Nazism the determinism of race. But the idea of men and women as the slaves of history runs athwart the deepest human instincts. Rigid determinism abolishes the idea of human freedom—the assumption of free choice that underlies every move we make, every word we speak, every thought we think. It abolishes the idea of human responsibility, since it is manifestly unfair to reward or punish people for actions that are by definition beyond their control. No one can live consistently by any deterministic creed. The Marxist states prove this themselves by their extreme susceptibility to the cult of leadership.

More than that, history refutes the idea that individuals make no difference. In December 1931 a British politician crossing Fifth Avenue in New York City between 76th and 77th Streets around 10:30 p.m. looked in the wrong direction and was knocked down by an automobile— a moment, he later recalled, of a man aghast, a world aglare: "I do not understand why I was not broken like an eggshell or squashed like a gooseberry." Fourteen months later an American politician, sitting in an open car in Miami, Florida, was fired on by an assassin; the man beside him was hit. Those who believe that individuals make no difference to history might well ponder whether the next two decades would have been the same had Mario Constasino's car killed Winston Churchill in 1931 and Giuseppe Zangara's bullet killed Franklin Roosevelt in 1933. Suppose, in addition, that Lenin had died of typhus in Siberia in 1895 and that Hitler had been killed on the western front in 1916. What would the 20th century have looked like now?

For better or for worse, individuals do make a difference. "The notion that a people can run itself and its affairs anonymously," wrote the philosopher William James, "is now well known to be the silliest of absurdities. Mankind does nothing save through initiatives on the part of inventors, great or small, and imitation by the rest of us—these are the sole factors in human progress. Individuals of genius show the way, and set the patterns, which common people then adopt and follow."

Leadership, James suggests, means leadership in thought as well as in action. In the long run, leaders in thought may well make the greater difference to the world. "The ideas of economists and political philosophers, both when they are right and when they are wrong," wrote John Maynard Keynes, "are more powerful than is commonly understood. Indeed the world is ruled by little else. Practical men, who believe themselves to be quite exempt from any intellectual influences, are usually the slaves of some defunct economist. . . . The power of vested interests is vastly exaggerated compared with the gradual encroachment of ideas."

But, as Woodrow Wilson once said, "Those only are leaders of men, in the general eye, who lead in action. . . . It is at their hands that new thought gets its translation into the crude language of deeds." Leaders in thought often invent in solitude and obscurity, leaving to later generations the tasks of imitation. Leaders in action—the leaders portrayed in this series—have to be effective in their own time.

And they cannot be effective by themselves. They must act in response to the rhythms of their age. Their genius must be adapted, in a phrase from William James, "to the receptivities of the moment." Leaders are useless without followers. "There goes the mob," said the French politician, hearing a clamor in the streets. "I am their leader. I must follow them." Great leaders turn the inchoate emotions of the mob to purposes of their own. They seize on the opportunities of their time, the hopes, fears, frustrations, crises, potentialities. They succeed when events have prepared the way for them, when the community is awaiting to be aroused, when they can provide the clarifying and organizing ideas. Leadership completes the circuit between the individual and the mass and thereby alters history.

It may alter history for better or for worse. Leaders have been responsible for the most extravagant follies and most monstrous crimes that have beset suffering humanity. They have also been vital in such gains as humanity has made in individual freedom, religious and racial tolerance, social justice, and respect for human rights.

There is no sure way to tell in advance who is going to lead for good and who for evil. But a glance at the gallery of men and women in ANCIENT WORLD LEADERS suggests some useful tests.

One test is this: Do leaders lead by force or by persuasion? By command or by consent? Through most of history leadership was exercised by the divine right of authority. The duty of followers was to defer and to obey. "Theirs not to reason why/ Theirs but to do and die." On occasion, as with the so-called enlightened despots of the 18th century in Europe, absolutist leadership was animated by humane purposes. More often, absolutism nourished the passion for domination, land, gold, and conquest and resulted in tyranny.

The great revolution of modern times has been the revolution of equality. "Perhaps no form of government," wrote the British historian James Bryce in his study of the United States, *The American Commonwealth*, "needs great leaders so much as democracy." The idea that all people should be equal in their legal condition has undermined the old structure of authority, hierarchy, and deference. The revolution of equality has had two contrary effects on the nature of leadership. For equality, as Alexis de Tocqueville pointed out in his great study *Democracy in America*, might mean equality in servitude as well as equality in freedom.

"I know of only two methods of establishing equality in the political world," Tocqueville wrote. "Rights must be given to every citizen, or none at all to anyone . . . save one, who is the master of all." There was no middle ground "between the sovereignty of all and the absolute power of one man." In his astonishing prediction of 20th-century totalitarian dictatorship, Tocqueville explained how the revolution of equality could lead to the *Führerprinzip* and more terrible absolutism than the world had ever known.

But when rights are given to every citizen and the sovereignty of all is established, the problem of leadership takes a new form, becomes more exacting than ever before. It is easy to issue commands and enforce them by the rope and the stake, the concentration camp and the *gulag*. It is much harder to use argument and achievement to overcome opposition and win consent. The Founding Fathers of the United States understood the difficulty. They believed that history had given them the opportunity to decide, as Alexander Hamilton wrote in the first Federalist Paper, whether men are indeed capable of basing government on "reflection and choice, or whether they are forever destined to depend . . . on accident and force."

Government by reflection and choice called for a new style of leadership and a new quality of followership. It required leaders to be responsive to popular concerns, and it required followers to be active and informed participants in the process. Democracy does not eliminate emotion from politics; sometimes it fosters demagoguery; but it is confident that, as the greatest of democratic leaders put it, you cannot fool all of the people all of the time. It measures leadership by results and retires those who overreach or falter or fail.

It is true that in the long run despots are measured by results too. But they can postpone the day of judgment, sometimes indefinitely, and in the meantime they can do infinite harm. It is also true that democracy is no guarantee of virtue and intelligence in government, for the voice of the people is not necessarily the voice of God. But democracy, by assuring the right of opposition, offers built-in resistance to the evils inherent in absolutism. As the theologian Reinhold Niebuhr summed it up, "Man's capacity for justice makes democracy possible, but man's inclination to justice makes democracy necessary."

A second test for leadership is the end for which power is sought. When leaders have as their goal the supremacy of a master race or the promotion of totalitarian revolution or the acquisition and exploitation of colonies or the protection of greed and privilege or the preservation of personal power, it is likely that their leadership will do little to advance the cause of humanity. When their goal is the abolition of slavery, the liberation of women, the enlargement of opportunity for the poor and powerless, the extension of equal rights to racial minorities, the defense of the freedoms of expression and opposition, it is likely that their leadership will increase the sum of human liberty and welfare.

Leaders have done great harm to the world. They have also conferred great benefits. You will find both sorts in this series. Even "good" leaders must be regarded with a certain wariness. Leaders are not demigods; they put on their trousers one leg after another just like ordinary mortals. No leader is infallible, and every leader needs to be reminded of this at regular intervals. Irreverence irritates leaders but is their salvation. Unquestioning submission corrupts leaders and demeans followers. Making a cult of a leader is always a mistake. Fortunately, hero worship generates its own antidote. "Every hero," said Emerson, "becomes a bore at last."

The signal benefit the great leaders confer is to embolden the rest of us to live according to our own best selves, to be active, insistent, and resolute in affirming our own sense of things. For great leaders attest to the reality of human freedom against the supposed inevitabilities of history. And they attest to the wisdom and power that may lie within the most unlikely of us, which is why Abraham Lincoln remains the supreme example of great leadership. A great leader, said Emerson, exhibits new possibilities to all humanity. "We feed on genius. . . . Great men exist that there may be greater men."

Great leaders, in short, justify themselves by emancipating and empowering their followers. So humanity struggles to master its destiny, remembering with Alexis de Tocqueville: "It is true that around every man a fatal circle is traced beyond which he cannot pass; but within the wide verge of that circle he is powerful and free; as it is with man, so with communities." ◆

1

Discovering the Queen of Sheba

VIRTUALLY EVERYTHING THAT PEOPLE KNOW—OR THINK THEY KNOW—ABOUT the Queen of Sheba has its roots in a story told in the Bible—13 verses in 1 Kings 10, and several more in 2 Chronicles. These few words have given rise to the many legends and tales that have kept the name and spirit of the Queen of Sheba alive for more than 3,000 years. She was a leader whose combined intelligence, political understanding, and charisma were seemingly so powerful that they have endured through centuries—despite the fact that those centuries have hidden the details of her reign, her history, and even her physical remains under the desert sand.

Some say the Queen of Sheba never existed—she was a figment of the imagination of some anonymous biblical scribe,

Ancient History, Facts, and Educated Guesses

The Queen of Sheba is believed to have lived in the tenth century B.C.—truly ancient history. The story of her meeting with King Solomon, as reported in the Bible, was recorded centuries after that. Although there is information concerning her land, the Sabean kingdom, in later centuries, information about its early years are scarce. The "real story" of her life remains a historical mystery simply because it happened so long ago. For many historians, solving that mystery is part of the fun.

Although it often seems that history is a collection of undisputed facts, Will and Ariel Durant say in *Our Oriental Heritage,* "Most history is guessing." Some historians view finding the thread of truth as a challenge: "The historian," says Gaetano Salvemini, "has before him a jigsaw puzzle from which many pieces have disappeared. These gaps can be filled only by his imagination." Mark M. Krug says simply, "[T]he historian and the detective have much in common."

"A mere compilation of facts presents only the skeleton of History," says historian Hannah Farnham Lee. "We do but little for her if we cannot invest her with life, clothe her in the habiliments of her day, and enable her to call forth the sympathies of succeeding generations." The Queen of Sheba—a woman who had the daring to travel through the Arabian desert to challenge King Solomon, reputed to be the wisest king in the world, to a duel of wits—has left history a fascinating story that historians, storytellers, theologians, artists, archaeologists, and others have been breathing life into for centuries.

Her story is recounted in the sacred literature of three major religions—Judaism, Islam, and Christianity. In Ethiopia, the Horn of Africa, and the Middle East, she is a familiar person, still loved, honored, and revered. And some believe she may soon be making a personal appearance. Today, in the deserts of Yemen, archaeologists are digging for facts that can be used to "clothe" the bare bones of her story, filling in the details of the life of this mysterious woman who can arguably be said to have been one of the greatest female leaders in history, and certainly one of the most memorable.

and the legends about her are nothing but children's tales. In her book *From the Beast to the Blonde*, Marina Warner calls her "a legendary figure compounded of fantasy and scripture, seriousness and comedy. . . . She mixes the fairy godmother and the fool, the enchantress and the houri, the wise woman and the witch, the Sibyl and the granny. . . ." Others believe she not only existed, but she was the founder of a great dynasty of Ethiopian royalty. Still others think perhaps her story was based on lives and exploits of several great women leaders of her country, women whose names have since been lost to time.

Given this uncertainty, how is it possible to tell the story authentically of Makeda, Queen of Sheba? Most researchers start at the beginning, with the story as told in the Old Testament.

THE STORY OF SOLOMON AND SHEBA

The story of the Queen of Sheba's visit to King Solomon of Jerusalem, as recorded in the Old Testament, is a simple story that has inspired folktales, national histories, books, operas, popular songs, and more than a few movies. But what makes this story so compelling and exciting for historians and other researchers is that its very simplicity gives it the ring of truth. Unlike most Bible stories, this tale has no supernatural elements. God does not speak, angels do not appear, miracles do not happen. This absence of embellishment has led to the theory that it is the straightforward record of a trade agreement between two powerful nations, written down by one of Solomon's court scribes at the time it occurred and included in the Bible centuries later.

Here's what might have happened: The Queen of Sheba—Hebrew for Saba, a powerful merchant state in South Arabia—began to hear stories of a wise and powerful king of a desert nation whose capital just happened to be located in Jerusalem, on the crossroads of two major trade routes. The queen's country was rich in vital natural resources, including what would later be called "the gifts of the Magi": gold, frankincense, and myrrh. Always on the lookout for ways to expand her nation's

The Queen of Sheba kneels before King Solomon in this French painting. Hoping to secure treaty agreements, the Queen of Sheba set off on a diplomatic expedition to court the favor of King Solomon. Upon arrival, she discovered her counterpart was as wise as his reputation had suggested, and they soon developed a fruitful professional and personal relationship.

trade and trading partners, and to secure safe passage through the desert for her merchant caravans, she felt a visit to this king might be in order.

On a more personal level, she may have been intrigued by Solomon's reputation for great wisdom. She, too, had a reputation for wisdom. Perhaps she felt that they would be able to make an even better trading agreement if they established a mutually respectful relationship as rulers. An intelligent woman as well as a shrewd politician, she decided to test the king with some well-thought-out questions of her own.

After much planning, she put together an impressive caravan of camels and servants carrying the riches of her country. She led this caravan on a dangerous desert journey that would take months.

Perhaps to her surprise and pleasure, Solomon answered her questions correctly. She liked what she saw, and he liked what he saw. She presented her gifts to the king, and in return he gave her "all she expressed a wish for, besides those presents he made her out of his royal bounty"—a key phrase most agree was a code for an intimate relationship, and the basis for stories about the great romance between Solomon and Sheba.

And then, her purposes accomplished, she returned home. Her journey was a success: She had established good personal relations and good trading relations with King Solomon, who controlled her country's access to other tribes and nations across the great desert.

JOURNEY BACK TO BIBLICAL TIMES

By itself, the story of Solomon and Sheba has lasted for millennia. But, by itself, it only provides a small bit of information about her life and times. Those times, so long ago, were biblical times. According to *Harper's Bible Dictionary*: "The biblical period properly extends from at least the Middle Bronze Age (2000–1500 B.C.) to the Greco-Roman period of the first century A.D." The Queen of Sheba's reign begins near the beginning of that period, around the middle of the tenth century B.C. Although the evidence of the story as written in the Bible speaks of her journey to visit King Solomon, finding evidence to corroborate it has been difficult. Knowledge about Saba and its civilization is still sketchy, especially in its first few centuries.

It is known that when the Queen of Sheba went to visit King Solomon, Saba was a young and wealthy kingdom in South Arabia, and it was soon to get even wealthier. But no Sabean writings discovered so far mention a queen during the time she is thought to have lived. Was the entire story made up? Are the dates wrong? Or have researchers simply not dug deep enough into the historical record?

Archaeologists and other researchers continue to look for her tomb and feel they may be getting closer to finding proof of her life. As Nicholas Clapp says in his book *Sheba: Through the Desert in Search of the Legendary Queen*, "Now she's getting very real. Her civilization is unquestionably real." He is not alone in feeling this way. In 2001, Michael D. Lemonick and Andrea Dorfman noted in *TIME* magazine, "This state of historical ignorance [about the Queen of Sheba] may be about to end." Archaeologists working in the desert of northern Yemen are uncovering the ruins of an ancient Sabean temple complex called Mahram Bilqis, "the Queen of Sheba's Sanctified Place." As researchers continue digging deep into the sands, they hope that this temple, and other ruins nearby, may hold the answers to the many questions about the Queen of Sheba, her life, and her people.

TALES OF THE QUEEN OF SHEBA

The questions people ask about the Queen of Sheba are at least as difficult as the ones she asked King Solomon, and with fewer certain answers. Known by many names—Makeda, Bilqis, the Queen of Sheba, Nikaulis, and the Queen of Egypt and Ethiopia are just a few—she is very much alive in the hearts and imaginations of people around the world.

Her stories have been part of oral history for centuries. And in the telling, as with all folk legends, they sometimes become wildly embellished. The ancient Jews were perhaps the first to add details to the simple biblical story, and some of their many tales about her exploits have been recorded in Louis Ginzburg's *The Legends of the Jews*. Another version of her story can be found in the Koran (the phonetic spelling of the Arabic Qur'an, the sacred text of Islam), in Sura (Chapter 27, "The Ant").

In the Middle Ages, an Arabic storyteller compiled more fabulous details in *Qisas al-Anabiya* (*Tales of the Prophets*). In these tales, even more than in the Jewish stories, magic was a given. Here the Queen of Sheba, called Bilqis, has a human father—but her mother is a djinn, a magical spirit of Arabian folklore, like the genie in Aladdin's magic lamp. Over the centuries, as people told and retold the stories of her life, and others wrote them down, the details grew and changed. They were not always flattering. Various stories say she had hairy legs; others note her misshapen left foot (which looked, variously, like an ass's hoof or webbed like a goose's foot or cloven like a goat's hoof). She was a queen (of Sheba), a lover (of Solomon), a demon (Lilith)—idolized and adored and demonized.

She was also an important figure in the history of Ethopia. The *Kebra Nagast* (*The Glory of Kings*), believed to have been compiled in the fourteenth century, is the holy book of Ethiopian Christians and Jamaican Rastafarians. This mix of legend and tradition, history and myth, derived (according to the Columbia University Press) "from the Old Testament and the later Rabbinic writings and from Egyptian (both pagan and Christian), Arabian and Ethiopian sources." Here, her story comes full circle: Once again, as in the Old Testament, it is a historical narrative. She is Makeda, queen of Ethiopia and Saba, mother of Solomon's son, Menelik, the founder of an Ethiopian empire that would last almost to the end of the twentieth century.

In most of the West, however, the Queen of Sheba's story is told in a different way: as the story of an outsider. The resolve that led her to travel a great distance to question King Solomon makes some people suspect her motives. She is seen as a "tramp," or a woman who does not "know her place." She has been demonized throughout history—sometimes literally labeled a demon. Even today, many Americans think of the Queen of Sheba as nothing more than a good-looking woman who thought she was smarter than Solomon, hung around his

The Queen of Sheba's story is considered to be more of a myth than an actual historical account. Despite mentions in the Koran, the Torah, and the New Testament, physical evidence of the queen is rare. Archaeologists, however, have uncovered a temple that may be the key to proving Makeda's existence and once powerful reign.

palace, and had her way with him. She is frequently held out as a bad example: Many young girls have been scolded with the words, "Who do you think you are, the Queen of Sheba?"

Increasingly, however, the Queen of Sheba's good reputation is being restored in the West. Feminists champion her as a woman who, regardless of controversy over the details of her life, deserves to be honored as a great leader. And many people of color have embraced her as a great African queen, along with Cleopatra of Egypt and Candace of Ethiopia.

But this is where her story ends. It begins in ancient Arabia. As the term is used in the Bible, Arabia was a vague area that encompassed a desert peninsula—1,600 miles (2,600 kilometers) long—between the Red Sea, the Persian Gulf, and the Indian Ocean. It was a land of extremes: burning sun, blinding sandstorms, even snow in mountainous regions, and a more temperate climate near the coast. It was in this pleasant coastal region, at the southern tip of Arabia near the Red Sea, that Makeda ruled Saba.

2

Who Was the Queen of Sheba?

HER NAME WAS NOT SHEBA: THAT WAS THE NAME OF HER COUNTRY. SHE came from Saba (in Hebrew, Sheba), a kingdom in South Arabia known for its trade in important natural resources. The Old Testament story of her meeting with Solomon is told twice: in 1 Kings and 2 Chronicles. Both record only the barest of details. But for anyone who wants to know more about this intriguing female leader who traveled to Jerusalem "from the ends of the earth" (as the New Testament says of Sheba in Luke 42), it leaves a lot to be desired. Nonetheless, everything that is known about the Queen of Sheba must begin here.

The Queen of Sheba's Visit to King Solomon of Jerusalem

When the queen of Sheba heard of the fame of Solomon (fame due to the name of the Lord), she came to test him with hard questions. She came to Jerusalem with a very great retinue, with camels bearing spices, and very much gold, and precious stones; and when she came to Solomon, she told him all that was on her mind. Solomon answered all her questions; there was nothing hidden from the king that he could not explain to her. When the queen of Sheba had observed all the wisdom of Solomon, the house that he had built, the food of his table, the seating of his officials, and the attendance of his servants, their clothing, his valets, and his burnt-offerings that he offered at the house of the Lord, there was no more spirit in her.

So she said to the king, "The report was true that I heard in my own land of your accomplishments and of your wisdom, but I did not believe the reports until I came and my own eyes had seen it. Not even half had been told me; your wisdom and prosperity far surpass the report that I had heard. Happy are your wives! Happy are these your servants, who continually attend you and hear your wisdom! Blessed be the Lord your God, who has delighted in you and set you on the throne of Israel! Because the Lord loved Israel for ever, he has made you king to execute justice and righteousness." Then she gave the king one hundred and twenty talents of gold, a great quantity of spices, and precious stones; never again did spices come in such quantity as that which the queen of Sheba gave to King Solomon.

Moreover, the fleet of Hiram, which carried gold from Ophir, brought from Ophir a great quantity of almug wood and precious stones. From the almug wood the king made supports for the house of the Lord, and for the king's house, lyres also and harps for the singers; no such almug wood has come or been seen to this day.

Meanwhile, King Solomon gave to the queen of Sheba every desire that she expressed, as well as what he gave her out of Solomon's royal bounty. Then she returned to her own land, with her servants. (1 Kings 10:1–13, New Revised Standard Version)

As the Queen of Sheba planned for her trip to King Solomon's kingdom, she gathered various treasures and rare materials she knew would impress the monarch. In return, King Solomon fulfilled her every request during her stay, and also presented the queen with gifts from his own royal vault. Lavish banquets *(above)* were held in honor of Makeda and the special friendship she had with the King.

LOOKING AT THE CLUES

Who was the Queen of Sheba? The story recorded in 1 Kings leaves only a few clues. She seems to have been an intelligent woman ruler who probably lived in the tenth century B.C. (because this is when Solomon is said to have lived). Her country was wealthy, and its products were desired. She was a bold and adventurous traveler; a smart political leader; and a woman confident enough to question a king said to be the wisest in the world. These bare outlines hint at a fascinating life that has compelled authors, artists, and filmmakers, as well as archaeologists, historians, and scholars to dig for the truth.

Archaeology can be very helpful in sorting out the details of life lived in ancient times. But in the case of the Sabean queen, it has yielded little—particularly in comparison to what is known about other ancient rulers, such as the kings and queens of Egypt. Their tombs, and the many artifacts of ancient Egypt that have survived the centuries, have given historical researchers abundant information about their lives and times. It also helps historians to find texts from the person's time that corroborate the details of their lives: personal diaries, court records, the records of those who knew them or met them.

In the case of the Queen of Sheba, the only real record is from the Bible, and it is not echoed by any source contemporary with her life. In contrast to the well-researched Egyptian materials—pyramids and tombs, written records, and all the rest—the ruins outside the Sabean capital of Marib (also spelled Ma'rib) in present-day Yemen, where she is thought to have ruled, are only now being excavated, and the drifting desert sands make the process very slow. Although researchers are hopeful, they still cannot point to the tomb of the Queen of Sheba, let alone know in any scientific or factual way what her name was, how she came to power, what she looked like, who her parents were, what her life was like, what she was really thinking when she went to visit King Solomon in Jerusalem, and what happened after she returned home to her own land.

Despite these obstacles, people have never stopped trying to fill in the outlines of the Queen of Sheba's life. As people fell in love with the romance of Solomon and Sheba, they told the story over and over again. As the tales spread from country to country, century to century, they picked up ever more embellishments, until the outlines of her life have become vivid with colorful—often conflicting, sometimes outlandish—details.

WHAT WAS HER NAME?

During the centuries, the Queen of Sheba has been known by many names. In Jewish tradition she was sometimes called Malkath, which is simply the Hebrew word for queen. Writings in the *Zohar,* part of the medieval Kabbalah (a book of Jewish mystical teachings), called her Lilith, a demon in Jewish folklore. In Arabic traditions, she was Bilqis (also spelled Balqis, or Balkis). Ethiopia has a separate historical tradition for the Queen of Sheba, whom they revere as a great leader. There, she is called Makeda, which means "Greatness."

HOW DID SHE COME TO POWER?

In ancient times, women tended to become rulers in one of two ways: They were born into power, or they married into it. In a 2001 discussion on PBS radio's *The Connection,* Carole R. Fontaine, feminist scholar and professor of Hebrew Scriptures at Andover Newton Theological School, explained, "You could be the daughter of the king who just died, and you could marry

The Many Names of the Queen of Sheba

- In the Old Testament, where she first appears, she is simply called the Queen of Sheba.
- In the New Testament, where it is predicted that she will preside with Jesus on Judgment Day, she is called the Queen of the South.
- In Arabic folktales, she is Bilqis (or Balqis or Balkis).
- The first century A.D. Jewish Roman historian Flavius Josephus wrote of her exploits, calling her the Queen of Egypt and Ethiopia, and naming her Nicaula, or Nikaulis.
- In the Mediterranean she is called Black Minerva, after the Roman name for the Greek goddess Athena, and Ethiopian Diana, after the goddess of the hunt.
- In Ethiopia, she is Queen Makeda, "Greatness," the mother of a nation and the founder of a royal dynasty.

a very weak man and [then] you are the one who is really the power. Sheba seemed, in some of the Arabic materials, to have come into power that way."

Makeda is "a very present and real fact of Ethiopian history," says Ephraim Isaac, director of the Institute of Semitic Languages in Princeton, New Jersey, and that history puts precise dates on Makeda's life. Many Ethiopians believe she was born in 1020 B.C. in Ophir (a gold-producing country mentioned in the Bible that may be Saba), the daughter of Queen Ismenie. Makeda's father was said to be a chief minister to the king, who later became king himself. When her father died in 1005 B.C., Makeda became queen at the age of 15. She had a child, Menelik, with King Solomon, and her son succeeded her as king of Ethiopia. According to this history, she never married.

TRADITIONAL STORIES

Oral histories are stories passed down from generation to generation, losing some details and picking up others as they evolve. In Africa and the Middle East, oral traditions about Makeda are still evolving. These legends tell different tales of the queen's rise to power.

In Arabic tradition, a man named al-Himyari, was a handsome and resourceful counselor to an evil king. He fell in love with a beautiful djinn (or genie) named Umaya, and they had a daughter, Bilqis. Unfortunately, when al-Himyari was in the city advising the king, Umaya died, leaving Bilqis on her own in the desert, to be raised by gazelles and djinns. She was later reunited with her father, killed the king, and was acclaimed as a hero and made queen by popular demand.

Ethiopian oral history differs from its official history. In this story, Ethiopia was ruled by the feared and monstrous Wainaba, the snake king. The people make an offer to Makeda's father, Angabo: If he could kill Wainaba, they would make him king. Knowing that the great serpent ate a thousand goats every day, Angabo feeds it a poisoned goat. When Wainaba dies, Angabo comes to power. On his death his daughter, Makeda, becomes queen.

MORE THAN ONE QUEEN?

Some experts believe that the conflicting details in stories about the Queen of Sheba may be due to the fact that her legend is actually based on a combination of women leaders of the time. Although it was by no means common for women to rule in these male-dominated cultures, it was not unheard of.

According to the Web site Worldwide Guide to Women in Leadership, "Some Egyptian Queens are believed to have governed from around 3000 B.C.," and a number of women occupied positions of power around the time of the Queen of Sheba. According to archaeologist William Glanzman, who heads the team excavating Mahram Balqis, "We have many queens from the region. . . . [Each] may have contributed in some small way to [the image of] the mysterious and enigmatic Queen of Sheba."

WHAT DID SHE LOOK LIKE?

Most people throughout history have agreed on this point: The Queen of Sheba is universally believed to have been a strong and beautiful woman. But exactly what she looked like is a matter for debate.

Although centuries of Western art portrayed her as a white European monarch, the Queen of Saba (a kingdom that included southern Arabia and parts of Ethiopia) was almost certainly a woman of color. Scholars debate whether she was an Arab or an African. Some claim her as a purely African queen, and cite the line from the Song of Solomon attributed to her: "I am black and beautiful" (Song of Songs 1:5, NRSV). Ethiopian art does indeed represent her as a beautiful black African woman; Middle Eastern art usually portrays her as an Arab. According to the *Encyclopedia Britannica*, "The racial affinities of the ancient Yemeni peoples remains unsolved." In other words, no one really knows.

Most experts agree that at one time Ethiopian and Sabean societies shared a culture, and both can lay claim to the Queen of Sheba. "South Arabia and Ethiopia were separated only by a narrow body of water," explains Alice Ogden Bellis in *Helpmates, Harlots, and Heroes: Women's Stories in the Hebrew Bible*. "The South Arabians and Ethiopians interacted culturally on a regular basis. Ethnically they were closely related."

One story that persists about the Queen of Sheba throughout countries in the East and the West has to do with the appearance of her legs and feet. Hebrew and Arabic tradition both mention that the Queen of Sheba had hairy legs—which apparently did not bother the queen, but did disturb Solomon.

A Short List of Ancient Women Leaders

This is a short list of women who ruled at about the same time as the Queen of Sheba (ca. 970–940 B.C.). Many others came before her and after her.

ca. 993 B.C. Queen Nodjemet of Egypt

990–969 B.C. Governor of Foreign Countries Queen Nesihonsu of Egypt, vicereine of Nubia

990–before 969 B.C. Politically influential Queen Isetemachbit IV of Egypt

981 B.C. Regent Dowager Queen Ishaq of Thama (Arabia)

ca. 984 B.C. Queen Duat-Hathor Henuttauy II of Egypt

873–843 B.C. De facto coruler Queen Jezebel of Israel

Source: Adapted from Worldwide Guide to Women in Leadership www.guide2womenleaders. com. (January 10, 2007)

A story in *Legends of the Jews* tells of the king and queen's first meeting: Solomon's servant Benaiah brings the queen to Solomon's palace, where the king has arranged to meet her in a specially constructed glass house. The queen "thought the king was sitting in water, and as she stepped across to him she raised her garment to keep it dry. The king noticed hair on her bare feet, and he said to her: 'Thy beauty is the beauty of a woman, but thy hair is masculine; hair is an ornament to a man, but it disfigures a woman.' " Wisely, the queen ignored this comment and smoothly responded, "I have heard of thee and thy wisdom; if now I inquire of thee concerning a matter, wilt thou answer me?" Then, according to this telling, she asked the king to answer 22 extremely difficult questions.

Arabic tales also tell this story, but it takes place later in her visit to Jerusalem. One day, Solomon hears gossip from the djinns that Bilqis is really a djinn. The proof, they say, is that she has hairy legs and one of them ends in a hoof rather than a foot. Solomon must see for himself if this is true, so he puts a glass-covered fishpond between himself and Bilqis. The queen, thinking she must walk through water to get to the king, lifts her skirts to cross, revealing her legs and feet. Solomon sees that her legs are indeed covered in hair, but her foot is merely misshapen. (In Ethiopia, this deformity is said to be the result of a childhood bite by her pet jackal.) The sight of her legs causes him to invent what has been called the first depilatory cream, a hair remover made of slaked lime (calcium oxide mixed with water) and ash.

WISE, WEALTHY, AND POWERFUL

Once thing, however, is certain: Makeda was a force to be reckoned with. Fontaine says bluntly, "She's a smart woman in a man's world and she's there dealing for her people." This queen who was determined to test the wisdom of the king reputed to be the wisest on earth was herself a woman of intelligence and wisdom. In the *Kebra Nagast,* Makeda says that wisdom is "far

Soon after her visit in King Solomon's kingdom, Makeda discovered that she was pregnant. In a tribute to his father, she named her son Menelik, which means "Son of the Wise."

better than treasure of gold and silver." During her rule, she seems to have focused her wisdom and intelligence on ensuring Saba's prosperity.

Makeda is said to have ruled Saba in the tenth century B.C., an era of powerful men. In Egypt, King Siamun built or added to many monuments of ancient Egypt, including the Temple of Horus and the Temple of Amun. In Israel, King David died and his son, Solomon, became king of a united Israel, and was engaged in building the First Temple in Jerusalem. Twice destroyed and once rebuilt since then, its walls still stand. Nearly 1,500 miles (2,414 km) from Jerusalem, in South Arabia, Saba was just emerging as a prosperous merchant kingdom that would last for centuries. Today, ancient Saba's enormous buildings have fallen into ruin or been buried deep under the desert sands. But during its lifetime Saba, rich in natural resources and fortunate in location, was a kingdom to reckon with.

Saba, the Biblical Land of Sheba

THE QUEEN OF SHEBA, SAYS MARINA WARNER IN *FROM THE BEAST TO THE Blonde,* embodies the land she rules: "The imaginary geography of Saba can be mapped much more precisely than its historical position. From readings of the Bible itself, Sheba, or Saba, represents the far south, redolent of luxury and sensual pleasures."

According to the Koran 34:15, "Sheba's homeland used to be a marvel, with two gardens on the right and the left." Like any good piece of real estate, Saba owed a lot to its location. At the southern tip of Arabia, it encompassed present-day Yemen on one side of the Red Sea channel and parts of present-day Ethiopia and Eritrea on the other.

At first glance, it may seem odd that the Sabean kingdom was able to jump the Red Sea. But according to Ephraim Isaac, such an alliance was not unusual in ancient times. As he explained in an interview on PBS radio's *The Connection* in 2001, "Lands at those times separated by sea were more unified than those separated by deserts and mountains." And for a simple reason: It was easier to sail across a narrow channel than to travel across the rugged mountains or the brutally hot desert. So these lands, both rich in natural resources, formed a unified state connected by trade and politics.

The Great Dam

The Great Dam of Marib—actually, a series of dams—is thought to be the oldest artificial dam. This enormous packed earth dam—the largest dates to the fifth century B.C.—was a stunning feat of ancient engineering, and it has been called one of the miracles of the ancient world.

Marib had prospered even before the Queen of Sheba's time—due, in large part, to an ingenious dam that, according to Nicholas Clapp's *Sheba*, made Marib "a major city with an agricultural base that was both dependable and bountiful." About 1500 B.C., the Sabeans blocked the Wadi Adana, a dry riverbed that ran past Marib, allowing the monsoon rains that fell in the mountains to flow into the dam and be used to irrigate an estimated 24,000 acres (9,600 hectares) of land—likely enough cropland to feed Marib's estimated population of 20,000 during Makeda's rule. All that water also allowed the building of Marib's two large artificial oases, filled with palm trees and gardens—a fitting place for a queen.

The last of a series of great dams collapsed A.D. 570. In 1987, a modern dam was built that made ancient farmlands usable once again.

The heart of the kingdom—in present-day Yemen, about 100 miles (160 km) inland from the Red Sea coast—was nestled into an almost perfect zone. Yemen is home to the highest mountains in the area, as high as 12,008 feet (3,660 meters). With high mountains on one side and the harsh desert on the other, it was not an easy target for raiders. The sea had a moderating effect on the hot desert, and monsoons created dependable rainfall and fertile soil. Saba's comfortable, moist, and temperate climate was known throughout the ancient world. The ancient Greeks called Saba Arabia Eudaimon, "Arabia the Blessed," and the Romans called it Arabia Felix, "Happy Arabia."

Its landscape, too, was fortunate. At the edge of the seemingly endless sands of the desert, Saba's views were made lively by green hills, high mountains, and valleys. Rivers ran down from the mountains, and over the centuries the Sabeans helped nature along by building a succession of huge dams—great engineering projects of the ancient world that dated back to 2000 B.C. The dams pooled the water that would have otherwise run off, unused, and created a sophisticated water system to irrigate thousands of acres of crops.

INCENSE

The Sabeans also owed their fortunes to three related factors. First, they had a wealth of natural resources—chiefly gold, and the sought-after incense ingredients frankincense and myrrh, among other spices (including saffron and cumin). Second, their strategic location on the so-called Incense Route—near the Red Sea coast, between Arabia and Africa—meant they were perfectly positioned to trade goods with countries thousands of miles away, by land and sea. Third, a new invention—a saddle that allowed camels to carry heavy weights for long distances—allowed the Sabeans to ship their goods more easily to distant countries across the desert. Combined, these factors allowed Saba to become an important player in the lucrative

The great Sabean Dam in Yemen *(above)* directed monsoon and river waters to agricultural fields and lush oases. While the ancient, earthen dam is considered a great feat of engineering for its time, it soon deteriorated from neglect and an economic shift from farming to sea trade. A modern dam was built in 1987 to provide water to the arid region.

incense trade. In fact, the kingdom dominated the international spice and incense market, comparable to dominating the world's oil industry today.

Incense was in daily use in Saba, Greece, Rome, Babylon, Jerusalem, Egypt, and elsewhere. It had many uses. People burned it in temples, in the hope that its white smoke would carry prayers to the gods. They threw it on funeral pyres as an offering to the gods and as a way to mask the odor of burning bodies. In these days, before indoor plumbing and sanitation facilities, it was also used in homes as an air freshener and to kill insects in clothes.

They even used incense spices medicinally. According to Kitty Morse in *A Biblical Feast*, frankincense was "given as an antidote for poison, and as a cure for chest pains, hemorrhoids, and paralysis. Myrrh . . . was used in preparing bodies for burial, for healing ear, eye and nose ailments, and for inducing menstruation." In the tenth century A.D., Persian physician and philosopher Avicenna (Ibn Sina) suggested its use for curing tumors, ulcers, vomiting, dysentery, and fevers. According to the first century A.D. Greek physician and pharmacologist Dioscorides, myrrh was also used against dysentery and worms and in wine making. In Egypt, myrrh was used to mummify the dead, and the burned resin was used to make the dark kohl makeup women used to outline their eyes.

In the fifth century B.C., Greek historian Herodotus wrote of South Arabia: "This is the one country in the world where frankincense grows, and myrrh, and cassia, and cinnamon and laudanum . . . the whole country exhales a more than earthly fragrance." This is the air the Queen of Sheba inhaled every day of her reign, and the scent of life in the great Sabean cities Marib and Sirwah. The list of uses for frankincense and myrrh gives a feeling for what life might have been like for the Sabeans. In a time centuries before germ theory, hospitals, and Western medicine, people looked for cures closer to home. And in a world without refrigeration or sanitation, their sweet, heavy scent filled the air of Saba's outlying farming communities and great cities, masking the more earthy odors of daily life.

A THRIVING CIVILIZATION

In the tenth century B.C., Saba was peaceful and, by all indications, had a thriving civilization. The Sabeans worshipped many gods, they built enormous buildings and created many objects that still survive, used their sophisticated irrigation system to grow crops to feed a large population, and had their own spoken and written language.

LANGUAGE

The Sabeans spoke a now-dead language, Sabean, which was related to Arabic and Ethiopian. They also had a written language, known today as Epigraphic South Arabic (ESA), and they left thousands of inscriptions for archaeologists and epigraphers (people who study and translate inscriptions). The Sabeans seem to have been a literate people. They wrote their names on ceramic vessels; they wrote pleas to the gods in their temples; they left inscriptions on monuments and buildings; and they kept records on plant- and animal-skin-based papers, recording religious ceremonies, building, and property papers, construction records, and much more.

A WEALTHY ELITE

Archaeological finds, including bronze and alabaster statues, monumental buildings, gold jewelry, incense burners, and carvings, give hints about the daily life of Sabeans. One carving that shows two household scenes, for example, shows a woman wearing a long dress. She is sitting on a chair, with her feet resting on a stool, and she is playing a lyre (a stringed instrument). A young girl stands near her, and another girl is holding a drum. In the next scene, a woman lies on a couch and seems to be speaking to an attendant. The scene is inscribed with a warning from the owner: "Image of Ghalilat, daughter of Mafaddat and may Athtar [a protective deity of the Sabeans] destroy he who breaks it."

The woman who issued this objective was very likely part of Saba's wealthy elite, from which the Queen of Sheba—whether she was a hereditary ruler, or married into the monarchy—

undoubtedly came. According to the *Jewish Encyclopedia*: "The great families [of Saba], which evidently possessed large landed estates, had castles and towers." Heavy gold jewelry, engravings like the one just described, and other artifacts have been found that suggest the wealthy lived a life of ease and enjoyment. Sabean women are also believed to have enjoyed relative social equality with men. If so, it is not so difficult to believe that a strong, intelligent woman like Makeda would have been able to lead at the full height of her powers.

What *Are* Frankincense and Myrrh?

Frankincense and myrrh—vital ingredients of incense—were once valuable commodities. Today, most people know them as "the gifts of the Magi," but few know what they actually are.

Frankincense and myrrh are dried and prepared sap from trees that grow in the area of ancient Saba and virtually nowhere else in the world. Frankincense is obtained from the shrubby *Boswellia sacra,* which only grows in South Arabia. Myrrh is the resin of the tree *Commiphora myrrha,* which grows in South Arabia and Somalia.

These resins have been harvested in more or less the same way for thousands of years. In one technique, the bark is cut with a knife, and the sap that oozes out is allowed to dry. In another technique, the tree is debarked and the sap is removed and refined, until all that is left are the gummy yellow drops of resin. When the resin drops are dry and hard, they can be burned as is or powdered and combined with other ingredients to make incense.

Today, frankincense and myrrh are still used, but primarily to make incense rather than to cure disease. In Ethiopia today, frankincense is a vital and indispensable part of church services.

Religion

With notable exceptions, chiefly the Israelites, most ancient peoples were polytheists—they worshipped more than one god. The Sumerians, Egyptians, Greeks, and Romans all had pantheons of deities. The Sabeans were no exception. According to the *Catholic Encyclopedia*: "The [Sabean] inscriptions commemorate gratitude for success in arms, 'man-slaying,' health, preservation, safe return, booty, and rich crops. Worshippers offer to the gods themselves and their children, register vows, and attest their fulfillment."

Louis Ginzburg's story "The Queen of Sheba," in *Legends of the Jews,* portrays a small but striking moment of her spiritual life in Saba: "It was morning," he says, "and the queen had gone forth to pay worship to the sun." She was probably paying homage to Shams, the Sun god. At night she would send her prayers to Almakah (also spelled Almaqah, or Ilumquh), the Moon god, and the god of agricultural fertility.

She may well have worshipped Almakah at Mahram Bilqis, "the Queen of Sheba's Sanctified Place." This enormous complex is the earliest known Arabian temple, and it may even be where she is buried. It was located across the Wadi Adana, near the great city of Marib, called in ancient times "the Garden of Two Paradises."

THE CITIES OF SABA

Marib, the capital of Saba in South Arabia, was one of three major Sabean cities. Sirwah, nearby, may have been an earlier capital. The queen's capital city in Ethiopia was Aksum (also spelled Axum), which would later develop into a powerful state in its own right.

Marib

"Marib was for centuries the political, economic and religious center of the once-mighty kingdom of Sheba, referred to in the

Once a great citadel, the city of Marib was the capital of the Sabean kingdom. Located directly on the incense trade route, Marib was the economic, religious, and cultural center of the state. Surrounded by orchards fed by the waters from the Sabean Dam, the city of the Queen of Sheba was a virtual paradise in ancient times. Although modern-day Marib is much more muted and modest, relics of the old kingdom stick out from under the sand, waiting to be revealed once again.

Torah, the Bible and the Koran," says archaeologist Burkhard Vogt (in a December 22, 2000, article from BBC News). In the Koran, the Queen of Sheba's capital is called Kitor, "the Garden of Two Paradises," where the water from a dam feeds so many palm trees that citizens are always shaded from the sun's heat; and so rich that "gold was no more valuable than dust, and silver was like mud in the streets." Kitor is believed to have been Marib.

Marib was built on a plain at almost 4,000 feet (about 1,219 m), just 140 miles (225 km) from the Red Sea and looking down on the edge of the eastern high desert, 75 miles (120 m) east of Sana (also spelled 'San'ā', or San'aa), the capital of Yemen.

Today, the ruins of Old Marib are studied by archaeologists and taken home in snapshots by tourists. But in ancient times, this bustling city was an important meeting point for caravans traveling the Incense Route, and it was a place of power for the Sabean kingdom. To speak the name of the great city was to conjure up a vision of "riches beyond belief."

Marib's city walls enclosed about 275 acres (110 hectares) and may have been home to 20,000 or more citizens—a large city in those days, filled with people, their animals, and life being lived. Lush and green, the city was filled with art, gardens, courtyards, markets, and ancient mud-brick tower houses (similar to the tower houses that still exist in modern-day Yemen) more than 80 feet (24 m) high and comprised of six to eight stories. Elite Sabeans could look over the city from the top floors, enjoying their unobstructed view of Happy Arabia.

Sirwah

Sirwah, about 25 miles (40 km) west of Marib, was built in a valley encircled by mountains. It may have been Saba's capital before Marib. At an altitude of about 5,000 feet (1,524 m), its naturally cooler climate was the logical place for the queen to live in summer, a refreshing escape from the more humid temperatures at lower elevations.

Aksum

Makeda would have to sail across the Red Sea channel to reach her African capital, Aksum. This green and fertile region, at

7,200 feet (2,194 m) above sea level, was home to elephants, rhinoceroses, and other animals unknown in South Arabia.

Aksum became a powerful kingdom centuries after the Queen of Sheba's day, but little is known about its earlier years.

Strabo on Saba

In A.D. 22, in his work *Geography,* the Roman writer Strabo had this to say about the Sabeans of his time:

> The country of the [Sabeans], a very populous nation, is contiguous [most of modern Yemen], and is the most fertile of all, producing myrrh, frankincense, and cinnamon. . . . There are snakes also of a dark red color, a span in length, which spring up as high as a man's waist, and whose bite is incurable. On account of the abundance which the soil produces, the people are lazy and indolent in their mode of life. The lower class of people live on roots, and sleep on the trees. The people who live near each other receive, in continued succession, the loads of perfumes and deliver them to others, who convey them as far as Syria and Mesopotamia. . . . The people cultivate the ground, or follow the trade of dealing in aromatics, both the indigenous sort and those brought from Ethiopia; in order to procure them, they sail through the straits in vessels covered with skins. There is such an abundance of these aromatics, that cinnamon, cassia, and other spices are used by them instead of sticks and firewood. . . . By the trade in these aromatics both the Sabaeans and the Gerrhaei have become the richest of all the tribes, and possess a great quantity of wrought articles in gold and silver, as couches, tripods, basins, drinking-vessels, to which we must add the costly magnificence of their houses; for the doors, walls, and roofs are variegated with inlaid ivory, gold, silver, and precious stones. . . .

According to archaeologist Stuart Munro-Hay, a 1974 excavation found Sabean inscriptions here, along with "stone altars, elegant limestone female statues dressed in pleated robes, [and] canopied thrones decorated with carved ibex." Aksum is still the heart of worship for Makeda in Ethiopia.

THE FALL OF SABA

Saba seems to have enjoyed a peaceful era during the eleventh and tenth centuries B.C. Good trading partners, good fiscal and political management, plentiful crops, and perhaps fewer military expenditures helped make Saba the wealthiest and most powerful of five trading states in pre-Islamic southern Arabia—then, and for centuries afterward.

But the same fortunate location that brought all that prosperity let Saba down beginning in about the sixth century B.C., when the Incense Route was rerouted away from the kingdom. Their economy was based on that trade, so the sudden change in fortune put the Sabean civilization into a decline from which it would not recover.

In Makeda's time, with Saba's valuable natural resources that were in great demand throughout the ancient world, the prospects for the country's success in international trade were great. Makeda would have had every reason to believe she could be successful in trading ventures if she could secure safe passage for Saba's gold, gems, and spices through the desert that began on the edge of the Sabean kingdom and stretched for thousands of miles through Arabia. When she heard about King Solomon, whose kingdom was centered in the strategically located town of Jerusalem, she prepared to make a deal that is still being talked about more than 3,000 years later.

A Dangerous Desert Journey

"WHEN THE QUEEN OF SHEBA HEARD OF THE FAME OF SOLOMON, . . . SHE came to test him with hard questions. She came to Jerusalem with a very great retinue, with camels bearing spices, and very much gold, and precious stones," says the Old Testament. But how did the fame of Solomon, from far away Jerusalem, reach Saba, more than a thousand miles across the desert?

Communication over long distances in the ancient world depended on messengers. People might send letters to one another, or travelers to distant lands would tell the people at home what they had seen. According to Ethiopian history, as recorded in the *Kebra Nagast,* the messenger was a merchant named Tamrin who had done business with King Solomon and was impressed by his fairness.

TAMRIN THE MERCHANT

According to the *Kebra Nagast* (22, 23), Tamrin was a wise and wealthy Ethiopian merchant, the leader of a caravan of 520 camels and with 370 ships at his command. When King Solomon wanted to build a temple in Jerusalem, he sent messages to all the merchants offering to trade gold and silver for building supplies. During this process, he heard about Tamrin and sent him a message asking for "red gold, and black wood that could not be eaten by worms, and sapphires." Tamrin got the message and brought Solomon the supplies he needed to build the great temple.

Tamrin's experience in Jerusalem did not end with the exchange of supplies for gold and silver. He stayed to watch as construction on the temple got started. Solomon assembled a large crew. He "appointed inspectors over the 700 woodmen who hauled the timber and the 800 masons who hewed the stone." According to Tamrin, the king wanted to learn all about the craft of building and working the wood and stone.

Tamrin was also impressed with Solomon's great wisdom and strength of character. "To those to whom Solomon had to give orders," said Tamrin, "he spake with humility and graciousness, and when they had committed a fault he admonished them [gently] . . . his words were sweeter than the purest honey; his whole behaviour was admirable, and his whole aspect pleasant."

Solomon not only paid Tamrin what they had agreed on, he also gave him "whatsoever he wished for in great abundance." When the merchant returned to Saba, he gave all of that to Makeda. He also told Makeda many stories about this wise king and his just and peaceful kingdom.

SOLOMON'S WISDOM

In recounting tales of Solomon's wisdom, Tamrin might have told the queen any one of a number of stories that are still told today. For example, when God came to the young

Solomon in a dream, asking what the new king most wanted, Solomon did not ask for wealth and power. Instead, he requested "an understanding mind . . . that I may discern between good and evil."

Perhaps the most famous story about Solomon's wisdom is the one commonly called "splitting the baby." One day, two

The Talking Hoopoe Bird

As the Queen of Sheba's legend evolved in Arabian and Jewish traditions, the messenger was neither of these. Instead, it was a talking hoopoe bird. This colorful crested bird of Europe, Asia, and Africa appears in many stories and paintings of the legend of Solomon and Sheba.

The Jewish Legend

In *Legends of the Jews*, Louis Ginzburg tells this story: One morning, when the Queen of Sheba was praying to the sun, a hoopoe bird flew over to her, and she saw that a letter was attached to its wing. It was a rather unsettling letter from King Solomon, inviting the queen to come visit him. If she came, he said, he would show her "great honor." But if she refused, "The demons will throttle you in your beds at night, while the beasts will slay you in the field, and the birds will consume your flesh." The queen took his threat seriously.

> [She] assembled all the ships of the sea, and loaded them with the finest kinds of wood, and with pearls and precious stones. Together with these she sent Solomon 6,000 youths and maidens, born in the same year, in the same month, on the same

women come to Solomon with a baby, each claiming that she is the mother. Solomon asks for a sword, saying that the only fair thing to do is to split the boy in two so each can have a portion. At this moment, the first woman begs Solomon to give the baby to the other woman rather than kill him, while the second woman cries out to "divide it" so neither will have the baby.

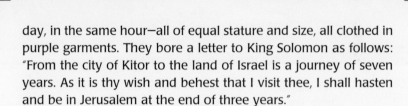

day, in the same hour—all of equal stature and size, all clothed in purple garments. They bore a letter to King Solomon as follows: "From the city of Kitor to the land of Israel is a journey of seven years. As it is thy wish and behest that I visit thee, I shall hasten and be in Jerusalem at the end of three years."

The Arabic Legend

The Arabic tale has another twist. In this long and detailed version, Solomon has a magic ring that gives him power over the winds, the djinns, and the animals and birds. The birds fly in formation to keep the sun from his eyes. One day, a ray of sun reaches Solomon's eyes because a single hoopoe has broken ranks. To save his life, the hoopoe tells Solomon that he has been to Kitor, and he tells Solomon about the riches of the city and the beautiful queen, Bilqis, who had overthrown a tyrant. Intrigued, Solomon sent the bird back to Bilqis with a letter commanding her to "surrender yourself to me."

In Kitor, the hoopoe told Bilqis about the powerful king. She, too, was intrigued, but she was also afraid and suspicious. She sent a messenger to make sure Solomon really was a prophet and not just a tyrant. The messenger confirmed that he was. Realizing that she could not resist him, Bilqis decided to journey to his kingdom and find out for herself what it was he wanted from her.

The judgment of Solomon is one of the most famous stories from the Bible, and used most often as an example of his wisdom. This famous depiction of the legend was painted in the seventeenth century by Nicolas Poussin and hangs in the Louvre.

Solomon gives the baby to the first woman, determining from her compassionate response that the baby must be hers.

Makeda "was struck dumb with wonder" at the things she heard about King Solomon, and she decided that she would make the long journey to meet him. Perhaps Makeda felt drawn to Solomon because she, too, was known for her wisdom. Before she sets out on her journey to Jerusalem, she gives this passionate speech (*Kebra Nagast* 24):

> I desire wisdom and my heart [seeks] to find understanding.
> I am smitten with the love of wisdom, and I am constrained
> by the cords of understanding; for wisdom is far better

than treasure of gold and silver, and wisdom is the best of everything that hath been created on the earth. Now unto what under the heavens shall wisdom be compared? It is sweeter than honey, and it [makes] one to rejoice more than wine, and it [illumines] more than the sun, and it is to be loved more than precious stones. And it [fattens] more than oil, and it [satisfies] more than dainty meats, and it [gives a man] more renown than thousands of gold and silver. It is a source of joy for the heart, and a bright and shining light for the eyes. . . . And as for a kingdom, it cannot stand without wisdom, and riches cannot be preserved without wisdom. . . . Wisdom is the best of all treasures.

In *Antiquities of the Jews* (Book VIII, Chapter 6:5), Flavius Josephus also writes about the queen's decision to visit Solomon. He stresses both Solomon's outstanding qualities, and the queen's sense of adventure and intellectual curiosity. She wanted "to be satisfied by her own experience, and not by a bare hearing," he says.

AN ANCIENT TRADE AGREEMENT

Makeda had another reason to visit Solomon beyond either fear or curiosity, and another reason for Solomon to desire Makeda's visit beyond her great beauty: It made good business and political sense to initiate a trade agreement between these two powers. According to the *Encyclopedia Britannica:* "The story provides evidence for the existence of important commercial relations between ancient Israel and Arabia."

Just before the Queen of Sheba's visit, the Old Testament (1 Kings 9:26–29) reports that King Solomon built a fleet of ships at the Red Sea port Ezion-geber. Hiram, the king of Tyre, was also involved in this venture. As Nicholas Clapp explains in *Sheba,* the ships "could have had little other purpose than sea trade south along the coasts of Africa and Arabia."

[L]arge or small, [the fleet] challenged the Sabeans to reach beyond their borders and establish a rival overland trade route. They had the goods, the transport, the demand. Everything was in place. But if they didn't move quickly, Judah and Tyre could sail to the shores of Arabia and . . . undercut Sabean control of trade to the north. Arabia's incense and spices were essentially valueless at their point of origin; fortune would smile on whoever initiated and controlled the trade, either by sea or land. 1 Kings 10 tells us it was the Queen of Sheba.

Saba had a wealth of natural resources to export, and a perfect location on the Incense Route. The high desert kingdom of Jerusalem was located on an important crossroads—the intersection of two major desert "highways." King Solomon stood a good chance of becoming even wealthier if he agreed to let merchants pass through his kingdom, collecting a tax from them for passage. Securing this route would be a win-win situation for both Makeda and Solomon. Again, Fontaine puts it bluntly: "You've got to go through Palestine to get anywhere—geographically, it's where the two flattest trade routes cross. And Solomon is the man to talk to."

A LONG JOURNEY ON THE INCENSE ROUTE

Makeda was unwilling to merely accept Tamrin's word that Solomon was a great and wise king, and she decided to see for herself. Josephus says, "If he could solve her riddles, she could verify his wisdom." But the journey the queen proposed to go on was at least as difficult as the questions she planned to ask the king.

Desert Dangers

She must have known the risks she faced. Leaving Saba, a virtual paradise of peace, wealth, and comfort, she proposed to go on a harsh and uncertain journey across the length of

Arabia to Jerusalem, almost 1,500 miles (2,414 km)—and so far away that Solomon's people thought of Saba as "the ends of the earth." She was headed for Jerusalem, a kingdom in the middle of the desert. She would have to lead her caravan—hundreds of camels, merchants, servants, and literally tons of trade goods, food, and water for the journey—across a desert baked by brutal heat and raked by sandstorms (in some seasons, torrential rains and flash floods) and human and animal marauders.

It's not unlikely that bandits, and enterprising tribal chieftains, might have attacked such a rich caravan. Watching for attack would occupy her guards. And the queen and her retinue would also need to avoid deadly snakes, like cobras and horned vipers, as well as jackals and scorpions.

The Incense Route

Fortunately, Makeda's route was not unknown. It was well traveled by the merchants of South Arabia, and it even had a name: the Incense Route.

The Sabeans exported their riches—which included frankincense, myrrh, spices, gold, ivory, pearls, precious stones, and textiles—overland by camel, to carry goods through Arabia and beyond, and by ship to India and other ports. They also received a variety of goods from traders along the road and from those traveling the Incense Route in reverse. According to the British Museum, an Assyrian text from the mid-eighth century B.C. reports that a caravan of "one hundred people from Tayma and Saba accompanied the caravan of two hundred camels," which carried iron, alabaster, and wool dyed a blue purple color.

Many tribal chieftains and desert magistrates got rich by taxing traders who wanted to pass safely through their kingdom or town. But merchants would rather not pay tolls to carry their goods from place to place. To evade these taxes, they kept adjusting their route. As a result, the precise path of the Incense

Route was always changing, and the fortunes of these desert towns and kingdoms went up and down regularly.

Nonetheless, thousands of tons of incense and thousands of camels and camel drivers traveled the route each year at its height. The Incense Route prospered until the second century A.D., when it became more profitable (and safer) to carry the spices on ships.

A Long Journey

The caravan's progress would depend not only on evading dangers, but on the health and strength of the camels, which could travel only 20 miles per day at best. At this pace, over a distance of almost 1,500 miles (2,414 km), her travels would take a minimum of 75 days—and likely much longer. (According to the first century A.D. Roman author, philosopher, and historian Pliny, every 20 to 25 miles (32 to 40 km), caravans on such a journey would stop to rest and water the camels in a city or town, in a desert oasis, or camp.)

Once Makeda's caravan reached Jerusalem, she and her retinue would stay for a while before heading back home. It would be a long time before she saw Saba again, and Jerusalem would be quite a different city than Marib.

THE QUEEN OF SHEBA ENTERS JERUSALEM

The Old City of Jerusalem today is the destination for pilgrims of three faiths, Jews, Christians, and Muslims, just as it was the destination 3,000 years ago for the Queen of Sheba. Jerusalem, in modern Israel, is really two cities: the New City and the Old City. The New City is a modern hub of culture and creativity: It houses a number of museums, two professional orchestras, a university, botanical gardens, a soccer stadium, shopping streets teeming with markets and shoppers and cafés, and a population of more than 700,000 spreading out into outlying neighborhoods and suburbs. The Old City contains some of the most sacred religious relics and shrines of three faiths, including King

David's tomb, the Mount of Olives, and the site of the Prophet Muhammad's ascent into heaven. In the tenth century B.C., however, Solomon's Jerusalem was a much different city.

Camels Make Long-Distance Trade Possible

The success of the Incense Route—and the Queen of Sheba's long and dangerous journey to Jerusalem—were made possible by the domestication of the camel and the invention of the load-bearing camel saddle, which allowed camels to carry heavy loads over long distances.

At first glance, the camel seems an unlikely hero in this story. The Arabian camel, or dromedary, is a large, gangly, web-footed, one-humped animal that stands between six and seven feet tall and may weigh up to about 1,500 pounds. But its odd characteristics make the camel perfectly adapted for desert survival. Webbed feet keep the enormous animal from sinking in the sand, and its nostrils are able to close to prevent sand from blowing in. A camel can store 30 gallons of water at a time, and it can go without drinking for more than two weeks. It can eat almost everything that grows in the desert (including thorns and plants too salty for other animals to eat), and people can burn its dung for fuel.

When the camel was first domesticated, desert people mostly used it as a source of meat. It was uncomfortable to ride, and the hump made it difficult to use as a pack animal, like the ass. But in about 1100 B.C., a new invention changed all that.

By the time of the queen's journey to meet King Solomon, the load-bearing camel saddle had turned the camel from solely a source of food into a beast of burden capable of comfortably carrying more than 300 pounds (136 kilograms) for long distances, although it is possible for them to carry 900 pounds (408 kg). Without the domesticated camel and its saddle, the Queen of Sheba's gift of "120 talents of gold"—estimated to weigh about 600 pounds (272 kg)—and "great quantities of spices and precious stones," not to mention the queen herself and her retinue of servants and bodyguards—would likely have remained safely in Saba.

The Western Wall *(above)*, located in Old Jerusalem, is one of the most revered sites in Judaism. It is the only remaining structure left standing after the destruction of the Temple of Solomon. People from all over the world travel to Israel and visit the Western Wall, where they write down prayers and wishes on small pieces of paper to slip into the cracks between the bricks.

Built high on a ridge in the Judean hills, Solomon's Jerusalem was surrounded by steep valleys. Dry and hot in the summer, cold in the winter, this Jerusalem was nothing like lush Marib.

In fact, Jerusalem could have fit inside Marib. According to Margaret Steiner's article "Jerusalem in the Tenth/Ninth Centuries B.C.," "Jerusalem was only a small town then, maybe 12 hectares large"—about 30 acres—"and it harbored certainly no more than 2,000 inhabitants. Maybe the Queen of Sheba would still have enjoyed her visit to Jerusalem, but I doubt that she would have been greatly impressed." Fontaine agrees: "At this point in time, Jerusalem is really a rather podunky kind of place."

The beautiful Queen of Sheba—heading a caravan of hundreds of camels, hundreds of people, and enormous amounts of precious goods—must have made a spectacular entrance into this desert outpost, home to just a fraction of Marib's population.

CHAPTER

5

Solomon
and Makeda

WHEN KING SOLOMON SAW THE QUEEN OF SHEBA'S CARAVAN ARRIVE
in Jerusalem after her long journey "from the ends of the
earth," with hundreds of camels and servants and extraordinary amounts of gold and spices, he could not help but be
impressed—not only by her beauty and wealth, but by her intelligence. Almost immediately, Makeda put the king to the test by
asking him what the Old Testament calls "hard questions."

HARD QUESTIONS

Just what these hard questions were, the Old Testament does
not say. Nonetheless, many over the centuries have filled in the
gaps. *Legends of the Jews* lists 22 questions.

Some are complicated theological riddles. For example, "A woman said to her son, thy father is my father, and thy grandfather my husband; thou art my son, and I am thy sister." Solomon correctly responds that "it was the daughter of Lot." And to Makeda's question "What land is that which has but once seen the sun?" Solomon answers, "The land upon which, after the creation, the waters were gathered, and the bed of the Red Sea on the day when it was divided." These questions, and other complicated tests, show that Makeda gave them a great deal of thought. (At least, they show that people credited her with the intelligence to match wits with King Solomon.)

Some of her "questions" involved quite a bit of preparation. In one test, she puts an equal number of boys and girls, all the same height and dressed in exactly the same way, before the king. She then asks him to determine which ones are girls and which

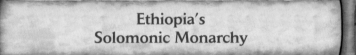

Ethiopia's Solomonic Monarchy

Ethiopia's hereditary dynasty, called the Solomonic monarchy, began with Menelik I, son of Queen Makeda and King Solomon, in the tenth century B.C. The dynasty lasted until 1974, when the last emperor, Haile Selassie—235 in a line of rulers who claimed to be directly descended from Makeda, the Queen of Sheba, and King Solomon—was deposed.

Haile Selassie made Makeda's place in Ethiopian history official in 1955, when he had these words written into the constitution: "The Imperial dignity shall be perpetually attached to the line of Haile Selassie I, descendant of King Sahle Selassie, whose line descends without interruption from the dynasty of Menelik I, son of the Queen of Sheba, and King Solomon of Jerusalem."

Makeda arrived at King Solomon's court with an army of camels and people, all carrying gifts of gold, and spices. Her trip across the desert impressed Solomon, and his respect for the queen grew as she presented him with a series of riddles. The Queen of Sheba's reputation for wisdom, endurance, and boldness is so famous the Greeks dubbed her, "The Black Minerva," after their goddess of wisdom.

are boys. In reply, he asks his servants to bring food—nuts and roasted corn. "The males, who were not bashful, seized them with bare hands; the females took them, putting forth their gloved hands from beneath their garments." Seeing this, Solomon knew the answer and correctly separated the girls from the boys.

In yet another kind of test, "The queen next ordered the sawn trunk of a cedar tree to be brought, and she asked Solomon to point out at which end the root had been and at which the branches." He told Sheba to put the tree trunk in the water, and saw that one end sank. From this he determined that the heavier end was the root, while the end that remained floating above the surface was the branch end. The queen was impressed: "Thou exceedest in wisdom and goodness the fame which I heard, blessed be thy God!"

But did Makeda really come all that way to ask King Solomon this series of brain teasers? Some think that it more likely that her questions were practical. According to Nicholas Clapp, they "almost certainly bore on long-range trade. Considering the geographical separation between Israel and Saba, what else could have been of issue?"

Saba's queen was now matched with arguably one of the most powerful monarchs of her time: Solomon, king of Israel, said to be the wisest man in the world. Yet she did not seem intimidated by him. She did not hesitate to cross the desert, and she did not waste any time getting down and asking him the difficult questions she had prepared. Part of her ease may have been cultural. As the queen in a land in which women enjoyed some equality with men (more, at least, than was common in many ancient cultures), she may naturally have considered herself more than equal to the task.

KING SOLOMON

King Solomon was the sixteenth son of the legendary King David, a poet, musician, and great military leader who united the 12 tribes of Israel into one kingdom and defeated the Philistines. He made Jerusalem the religious and political capital of his kingdom, which was bounded by the Euphrates River on the

A Feast Fit for a King and Queen

Solomon made a deep impression on Makeda, and so did his court, extravagant even in the middle of the rugged Judean hill region. The Old Testament says that "[w]hen the queen of Sheba had observed all the wisdom of Solomon, the house that he had built, the food of his table . . . [she was left breathless]." According to Kitty Morse, in *A Biblical Feast,* ordinary people in biblical times ate only a small amount of meat, but they had a bounty of fruits, vegetables, and legumes—olives and almonds, figs and dates, lentils and beans, melons and pomegranates, and bread, the staff of life. The elite, however, "enjoyed meat on a regular basis—goat, lamb, mutton, fatted calves, oxen, fowl (geese), wild goat, gazelle, antelope, deer, pigeon, dove, partridge, quail, milk and butter, cheese and yogurt."

The *Kebra Nagast* (25) reports that Solomon spared no expense in entertaining Makeda:

And he sent her food both for the morning and evening meal, each time fifteen measures by the *kori* [1 kor is about 30 bushels] of finely ground white meal, cooked with oil and gravy and sauce in abundance, and thirty measures by the kori of crushed white meal wherefrom bread for three hundred and fifty people was made, with the necessary platters and trays, and ten stalled oxen, and five bulls, and fifty sheep, without (counting) the kids, and deer, and gazelles and fatted fowls, and a vessel of wine containing sixty . . . measures, and thirty measures of old wine, and twenty-five singing men and twenty-five singing women, and the finest honey and rich sweets, and some of the food which he himself ate, and some of the wine whereof he drank. And every day he arrayed her in eleven garments which bewitched the eyes.

north and Egypt on the south. He declared Solomon to be his successor, even though he was not the oldest son.

Like his father, King Solomon was also a great leader and a poet, and he is sometimes credited with having written the Old Testament Book of Proverbs and Song of Solomon. Both Jewish and Islamic traditions also credit him with enormous natural and supernatural powers. According to *Legends of the Jews,* he "bore rule not only over men, but over the beasts of the field, the birds of the air, demons, spirits, and the spectres of the night. He knew the language of all of them and they understood his language." In the Koran, where he is called Sulayman, he is said to be a prophet.

Certainly, he seems to have been a visionary. Solomon's kingdom enjoyed peace and great power. He was a shrewd politician who was interested in developing industry at home (including copper mining and metal smelting) and expanding his kingdom's foreign trade connections. Geographically, he was in a perfect position to do this. Just as Saba was located on the Incense Route, near the sea and shipping possibilities, the city of Jerusalem sat right on the crossroads of two major trade routes through the desert. Anyone who wanted to trade with cities in any direction would have to pass through King Solomon's world.

ONE GOD

Clearly, Solomon was interested in the gold and spices Makeda had brought him—these vital natural resources were in short supply in his part of the world. Gold was as valuable then, as it is now. And the very expensive frankincense was especially welcome as an integral part of the daily spiritual life of the Jews. They used it as one of the four "sweet scents" in religious ceremonies, and it was also part of the weekly Sabbath offering.

Unlike the Sabeans, who recognized and worshipped many gods, the Jews under Solomon were developing into monotheists, people who worshipped one God above all, Yahweh. During her visit, the queen learned more about the God of Israel, even saying to Solomon (in 1 Kings 10:9), "Blessed be the Lord your God [Yahweh], who has delighted in you and set you on the throne of Israel!" She did not convert to Judaism, but she did give Yahweh, in Clapp's words, her "stamp of approval."

The Koran takes the queen's devotion a step further. Here, in the *sura* (chapter) called "The Ant," the king demands that she submit to his God. Eventually, she does, saying, "I submit with Solomon" to the one God.

In Ethiopian tradition, Makeda makes a crucial religious decision, saying (*Kebra Nagast* 28), "From this moment I will not worship the sun, but will worship the Creator of the sun, the God of Israel." This decision would result in a change of fortune for Solomon and the beginnings of a new religion and a new dynasty for her country.

A ROYAL ROMANCE

"Solomon marveled concerning the queen," says the *Kebra Nagast,* "for she was vigorous in strength and beautiful in form." Most people who know little else about the Queen of Sheba have at least heard that she had some sort of romance with King Solomon. This famous couple has been celebrated in story, song, books, operas, and movies, and painted on canvases, church walls, and wedding chests.

In the ancient Middle East, and in other parts of the world for centuries, it was not uncommon for intimate relations to be used to help seal political and tribal alliances—for example, a marriage between a prince of one country and a princess of another would unite the two politically. So it would not have been unusual for something along those lines to have happened here. But where does it say that in 1 Kings 10?

According to scholars, it's all in knowing how to read between the lines, and in understanding the implications of the original language. The words that have been translated "On coming to Solomon she opened her mind freely to him," for example, is used elsewhere in the Old Testament as a euphemism for sexual relations. From this small clue, storytellers wove intriguing tales of romance.

Seduction and Trickery

By the time the *Kebra Nagast* was compiled, the story of the romance between Solomon and Makeda had been transformed with much detail. It told the following story, which became the foundation of Ethiopian history.

Makeda had been visiting Solomon for some time, and was enjoying both his wisdom and his hospitality. He decorated a sumptuous room for her, with "purple hangings," carpets, marble, and precious stones. The room was permeated with the scent of perfume: He "burned aromatic powders, and sprinkled oil of myrrh and cassia round about, and scattered frankincense and costly incense in all directions" (*Kebra Nagast* 29).

Makeda, queen for six years before her journey across the desert, was a virgin. Determined that she would sleep with him, Solomon decided to trick her. One night, he served her a meal of "meats which would make her thirsty, and drinks that were mingled with vinegar, and fish and dishes made with pepper." It was a very long meal, and after many hours he sent his servants away. Eventually, the two were alone together. Because it was very late, he invited her to sleep in his chambers. She agreed, but only if he promised not to seduce her or take her "by force." Solomon agreed—with one condition: He would agree not to take her by force, but only if she swore that *she* would not "take anything by force that is in my house."

That night, they each went to sleep on opposite sides of the room. But earlier (knowing that sooner or later the spicy meal would make her thirsty), Solomon had his servants set out a bowl and pitcher of water. Sure enough, that night Makeda "was very thirsty indeed." Pretending to be asleep, Solomon watched as Makeda got up and picked up the pitcher—without asking his permission. Before she could drink the water, Solomon grabbed her wrist and accused her of breaking her oath. Because she was so thirsty, she agreed that he could be free from his part of the oath if he would just let her drink the water. After that, they slept together.

Through trickery, Solomon had taken Makeda's virginity. Apparently, the wise king felt guilty, because that night, he had a dream that, as a result of his "arrogance," God's "Sun" would desert Israel for Ethiopia, and "his soul became disturbed." When Makeda asked him to let her go home, he consented. He only asked that if their union resulted in a son, she should someday send him to visit his father.

Menelik I

Nine and a half months later, before she reached Ethiopia, Makeda gave birth to a son at Maibella (now in Eritrea) and named him Menelik. The boy grew up strong and handsome in Aksum—in fact, he looked just like King Solomon. At the age of 22, he left home to visit his father in Israel.

After a long visit, Menelik returned home—but he was not alone. He brought with him the Ark of the Covenant, the central sacred object of the Jewish people. This was a special box that contained the original stone tablets of the Ten Commandments that Yahweh had given to Moses. It was an extremely powerful object, in which Yahweh was said to live, and protecting it from harm was of utmost importance.

Solomon had by now finished building the Temple, presumably with the supplies he had gotten from Tamrin and from Makeda. In a special secure location within the Temple, the Holy of Holies, he installed the Ark of the Covenant. With the blessing of "the Angel of the Lord," Menelik stole the Ark, and brought it triumphantly back to Aksum. (It should be noted that biblical historians believe the Ark was somehow lost in 586 B.C., when the Babylonians sacked Jerusalem.)

When Solomon discovered the loss, he was devastated, but the people of Aksum rejoiced. Under Makeda, they had already

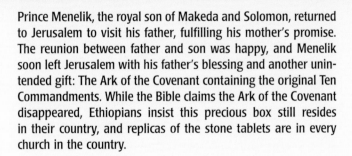

Prince Menelik, the royal son of Makeda and Solomon, returned to Jerusalem to visit his father, fulfilling his mother's promise. The reunion between father and son was happy, and Menelik soon left Jerusalem with his father's blessing and another unintended gift: The Ark of the Covenant containing the original Ten Commandments. While the Bible claims the Ark of the Covenant disappeared, Ethiopians insist this precious box still resides in their country, and replicas of the stone tablets are in every church in the country.

Chronology: The Queen of Sheba and King Solomon

ca. 1004 B.C. King David captures Jerusalem from the Jebusites and makes Jerusalem the capital of Israel.

ca. 980–950 B.C. Earliest and latest possible dates for the reign of King Solomon of Israel.

ca. 960 B.C. King Solomon begins to build the First Temple.

ca. 970–940 B.C. Earliest and latest possible dates for the Queen of Sheba's reign.

ca. 955–945 B.C. Queen of Sheba journeys north to Jerusalem.

Source: *Adapted from Nicholas Clapp,* Sheba: Through the Desert in Search of the Legendary King *(Boston: Houghton-Mifflin, 2001) and History.com.*

rejected their pantheon of gods, and now they felt the Ark had come to its rightful home. In fact, it fulfilled Solomon's dream that God's Sun would desert Israel for Ethiopia. Makeda decreed that she would step down as queen, and that her son would be King Menelik I, the first in a royal Ethiopian dynasty that would last for centuries.

"THEN SHE RETURNED TO HER OWN LAND"

During the Queen of Sheba's visit to King Solomon, she had accomplished quite a lot. She impressed him with the wealth of Saba and with her own power and wisdom. She established trade with his kingdom and probably secured his assurance of safe passage for Saba's caravans to points beyond Jerusalem. In his turn, King Solomon had established political relations with a powerful merchant state, increased the gold in his treasury, amassed a great deal of gemstones and incense, and made a powerful personal connection with an impressive, intelligent, and beautiful female monarch. Whether the union between the king and queen was a true romance or for more practical purposes, the union they established between Israel and Saba would last for a long time.

CHAPTER

6

Searching for the Queen of Sheba

IN THE ARTICLE "TREASURE FIT FOR A QUEEN," ABOUT THE BRITISH MUSEUM'S 2004 exhibit "Queen of Sheba: Legend and Reality," *The Christian Science Monitor* quotes British Museum curator St. John Simpson: "We can demonstrate the place, the economic truths, show what individuals of the time looked like. The only thing we can't provide here is the queen herself. [But] she rises from these objects, and her spirit floats through the show." But the question still remains: Where is the definitive proof that she really existed?

For centuries, few doubted that the scriptural stories of the Queen of Sheba were based on a real person. Unfortunately, there was no evidence of her life outside of these sources. By the late 1800s, as the quest of scientific proof in many areas of life began to become important, questions began to be asked. Where was her tomb? Where were the ancient writings that would confirm her reign? In the thousands of Sabean inscriptions, where was her name? With no physical evidence at all, how could it be proved that she existed?

Hoping to answer these questions, people began to search in earnest. Scientists are by definition skeptics who need irrefutable proof. University of Toronto museum studies professor Lynne Teather is hopeful. She believes that oral traditions and indigenous knowledge point to Makeda's last home and grave as being located in southwest Nigeria. "Each year both Muslim and Christian religious pilgrims come to this site in Ike-Eri to pray and honor the queen of Sheba," she says in a 2005 University of Toronto magazine article.

Archaeologist Ricardo Eichmann believes that no evidence that the Queen of Sheba was a "real historical person" has yet been found. "I don't say there definitely is no Queen of Sheba," he told *The Washington Post* in 2003. "I just say we have no physical or scientific evidence. . . . Bring me a piece of the Queen of Sheba and I will believe you."

Archaeology today is not just after the historical record, it is interdisciplinary. Teams of researchers from a variety of fields seek information that will help them form a 360-degree understanding of the cultures they are studying. Rather than merely searching for artifacts, for example, they may also consider "ecofacts." Organic evidence, such as plant life, seeds, animal bones, even insects, can tell much about a culture—what crops the people grew, what their diet was like, what animals might have lived nearby or been domesticated or even sacrificed in religious rituals, and so on.

Archaeology and biblical studies go hand in hand. "Archaeology . . . supplies the material evidence needed to elucidate the biblical text," explains *Harper's Bible Dictionary*. "Archaeology makes it possible to place the Bible in its original setting by providing a physical context in time and place." It is also hoped that

Scientists hunting for proof of Makeda are concentrating on areas in Yemen, the site of the kingdom of Saba, and Ethiopia. Inscriptions from Yemen were found relating the stories of the kings of Saba *(above)*, but definitive proof of the Queen of Sheba remains elusive.

archaeology will help scholars envision the physical space and cultural world in which the Queen of Sheba lived.

Today, a number of scientists and researchers are actively engaged in the search to learn more about ancient Saba and the Queen of Sheba. Most of their efforts are centered on Ethiopia and Yemen, the site of the ancient kingdom of Saba, where inscriptions in the ESA language of the Sabeans have been found.

ETHIOPIA: AKSUM AND YEHA

"The origin of Ethiopia is largely the origin of us all," says Javier Gozalbez in *Touching Ethiopia*. Often called "the cradle of mankind," Ethiopia has been in existence for more than 2,000 years. Lake Tana, in northwest Ethiopia, is the source of the Blue Nile River. Now landlocked, in ancient times Ethiopia also included the country that is now Eritrea, on the Red Sea coast opposite

The Falasha: Jewish Ethiopians

Ethiopian Christians credit the Queen of Sheba with bringing the monotheistic beliefs of Israel back home with her. But Ethiopia is also home to Ethiopian Jews: the Falasha, the "House of Israel." Like the Solomonic monarachy, they also trace their descent back to Menelik I. According to the *Encyclopedia Britannica,* they were "probably descended from local Agew peoples converted by Jews in southern Arabia, [and] they remained faithful to Judaism after the Ethiopian kingdom was converted to Christianity in the 4th century A.D." By 1992, almost all of them had left Ethiopia to emigrate to Israel. Only a few are left in Ethiopia today.

Saudi Arabia and Yemen. Among all the countries of the world, this country of varied terrain and beautiful landscapes is foremost in its view of Makeda as a real world leader.

The story of Ethiopia's—and Queen Makeda's—history can be found in the *Kebra Nagast,* the Book of the Glory of Kings, the holy book of Ethiopian Christians and Jamaican Rastafarians. This 117-chapter book is generally believed by historians to be a compilation of Ethiopian oral history dating to the fourteenth century. It was originally written in Ge'ez (the official language of the Ethiopian court and the Christian Orthodox church), and has since been translated into many languages. The *Kebra Nagast* added many details to the spare story of the Queen of Sheba and placed her in the realm of historic reality.

In Ethiopia today, the spirit of Makeda is very much alive. Her image can be seen on paintings in Christian churches and on paintings intended for sale to tourists. Her name graces businesses, such as Aksum's Queen of Sheba Elementary School and the Queen of Sheba Hotel. Throughout Ethiopia, her story has been told and retold, and it can still be heard in the everyday conversations of Ethiopians.

Aksum

The Queen of Sheba's ancient Ethiopian capital, Aksum, is still centered around her memory. Many Ethiopians believe that Aksum is where the Queen of Sheba was crowned and reigned. The United Nations Educational, Scientific, and Cultural Organization (UNESCO), which has declared Aksum a World Heritage Site, calls it the "heart of ancient Ethiopia."

A kingdom, and the capital city of Ethiopia from the first to sixth centuries A.D., trade in gold and ivory once brought wealth to the region. By the tenth century, however, Aksum had fallen into decline. Today, the many ruins outside the city attract tourists and archaeologists.

Archaeologist Stuart Munro-Hay writes in *Aksum: An African Civilisation of Late Antiquity* that "[o]ne text calls the city the 'royal throne of the kings of Zion, mother of all lands, pride of the entire universe, jewel of kings' ":

> Although no information survives in the legends about the ancient Aksumite rulers who really built the palaces and erected the giant stone obelisks or stelae which still stand in several places around the town, these monuments are locally attributed in many instances to Menelik or to Makeda, the queen of Sheba. . . . Such legends are still a living force at Aksum today; for example, the mansion recently excavated in the district of Dungur, west of Aksum, has immediately been absorbed into local legends as the "palace of the queen of Sheba."

Today, Aksum is described (in a July 2006 article in *Guardian Unlimited*) as "little more than a village, a sleepy jumble of whitewashed lean-to houses and small, half-built tourist hotels in northern Ethiopia." There is plenty for tourists to see, however. The building said to be Makeda's palace is located a short distance from town, and the St. Mary of Zion Church is purported to be the resting place of the Ark of the Covenant, which Menelik I brought home from Jersualem centuries ago. The current church building was built in 1665, but the site itself probably dates back to the fourth century A.D. A small building called the Chapel of the Tablet is said to house the Ark. But does it? Although many Ethiopians believe it does, the claim cannot be verified because the chapel is guarded day and night.

Yeha

Yeha, several hours by car from Aksum, is Ethiopia's earliest high-country civilization. In its Timeline of Art History, New York's Metropolitan Museum of Art says that the most famous relic of the South Arabian influence on the area is a 60-by-50-foot (18-by-15-m) stone structure "estimated to have been constructed around the fifth or fourth B.C.," and possibly two centuries earlier. According to Nicholas Clapp, one theory holds that

> Yeha's temple was a centerpiece of a Sabean outpost established for the same reason the Queen of Sheba may have journeyed to Jerusalem: to further trade in incense and spices. . . . Not far away at Cohito was a dam constructed along the lines of the Great Dam at [Marib]. At other sites, inscriptions and altars were dedicated to [Almakah], the moon god of the Sabeans.

YEMEN: MAHRAM BILQIS

The Republic of Yemen, located between Oman and Saudi Arabia, borders the Arabian Sea, the Gulf of Aden, and the Red Sea. The Old City of Sana, in the nation's capital, is located in a high mountain valley at 7,200 feet (2,200 m). It is famous for its multistoried rammed-earth tower houses, which have been described as looking like wedding cakes. Marib, once the capital of Saba, is now little more than a village on the outskirts of the desert. It is near here, however, at Mahram Bilqis—the site of a temple abandoned in the sixth century A.D., and almost erased by drifting desert sands—that an active community of scientists hopes to find conclusive evidence of the Queen of Sheba.

The Search

There has been interest in exploring the area around Mahram Bilqis for more than 150 years. In 1843, a French pharmacist named Joseph-Thomas Arnaud traveled to Arabia hoping to find the spices the Queen of Sheba brought to King Solomon. He did not find them, but the place he searched—an ancient Yemeni temple, Mahram Bilqis, "the Queen of Sheba's Sanctified Place" (also called the Awwam Temple, or Temple of Refuge)— would later prove to be a promising site for archaeologists.

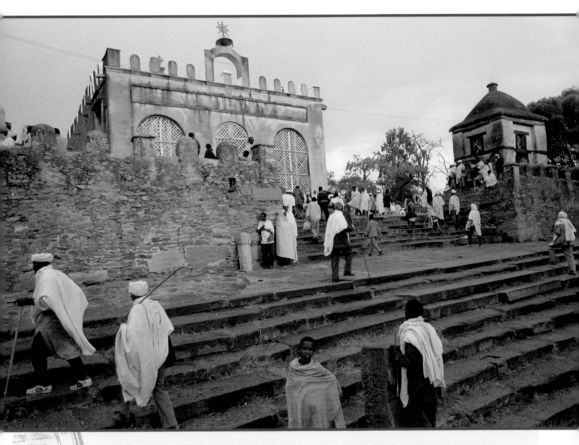

The Ark of the Covenant is believed by many to be housed in the St. Mary of Zion Church *(above)* in Ethiopia. The existence of the Ark is still debated, mostly because only one person, an appointed guardian, is allowed to see it.

According to the University of Calgary's modern chronology of Mahram Bilquis, the sanctuary was next explored in 1870 by a French scholar of Near Eastern antiquities, Joseph Halévy. In 1888, the German scholar Eduard Glaser described the site and recorded four important monumental inscriptions. In the 1940s, Nazih al Azm took the first photographs of the structure, and Egyptian archaeologist Ahmen Fakhry took more photographs and collected additional inscriptions.

In 1951, an American archaeologist, Wendell Phillips, began the first excavation of the ruins. In one short year, he made some exciting discoveries. According to the Web site of his sponsoring organization, the American Foundation for the Study of Man (AFSM), his team, "employing many local workers and dozens of teams of oxen, . . . unearthed 30 feet of sand revealing this grandiose hall with splendid bronze and alabaster sculptures." Unfortunately, that was virtually the last time anyone would see the excavated site. Phillips was forced to cease work and leave after just one year, chased from the area by political unrest just as he was reaching the layer of the temple he believed dated back to the Queen of Sheba's reign.

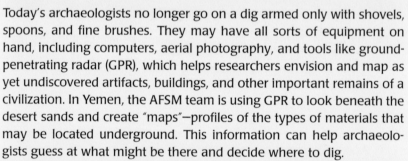

Looking Under Desert Sands

Today's archaeologists no longer go on a dig armed only with shovels, spoons, and fine brushes. They may have all sorts of equipment on hand, including computers, aerial photography, and tools like ground-penetrating radar (GPR), which helps researchers envision and map as yet undiscovered artifacts, buildings, and other important remains of a civilization. In Yemen, the AFSM team is using GPR to look beneath the desert sands and create "maps"—profiles of the types of materials that may be located underground. This information can help archaeologists guess at what might be there and decide where to dig.

The huge oval sanctuary of Mahram Bilqis, partially cleared by Wendell Phillips in his brief year's excavation, is buried under 26 feet (8 m) of sand in some places. This enormous quantity of sand—which nature often blows back after it is removed—is one reason why the excavation took as long as it did to get started, and why it is slow yielding its treasures. (It may take 15 years or more just to uncover the buildings.)

Something was salvaged, however: His colleague, Father Albert Jamme, was able to photograph and copy nearly 200 inscriptions from the ruins, mostly concerning offerings or entreaties to Almakah. Little work was done on the site for the next four decades. During this time, it was looted, and pieces were taken away for other uses.

For most of the twentieth century, experts dated civilization in the area to only 700 B.C., which would put finding Makeda's remains out of the question. (Although some of the ESA inscriptions that have been found are lists of reigning monarchs, none so far discovered mention a queen in Saba at the time she was thought to rule, around 950 B.C.) But that all changed in the late 1980s, when (as reported by *TIME* magazine's Michael D. Lemonick and Andrea Dorfman) "pottery shards from Wadi al-Jubah, not far from Marib, [were] found to be 3,500 years old. Suddenly, a wealth of other circumstantial evidence, both cultural and religious, made the Queen's existence seem a lot more plausible."

Into the Moon God's Temple

In 1998, at the request of Dr. Yusuf Abdullah, president of Yemen's General Organization of Antiquities and Museums, an international team of archaeologists and geologists sponsored by the AFSM finally resumed work. Today, under the direction of William Glanzman of the University of Calgary, they are actively excavating the site where Makeda may have worshipped Almakah.

The Wadi Adana separates the old walled city of Marib from the Mahram Bilquis temple complex. Using ground-penetrating radar and other high-tech tools, the AFSM team has discovered that the city and the temple were once linked by a causeway (a raised road over the Wadi Adana). Makeda might have walked, perhaps with a retinue of servants, from the lush green gardens of her capital into the hot summer sun and crossed the causeway to pray to Almakah in the Temple of the Moon.

As Makeda crossed the causeway, she would enter the portico of the temple, a roofed porch supported by tall, imposing limestone pillars. Inside, according to Sabean inscriptions, was an oracle, whom the queen and other citizens might have consulted for advice. Inscriptions found by the earlier expedition ask Almakah for protection against enemies and other favors.

The sanctuary itself is a huge oval measuring 314.3 feet (95.8 m) across, bounded by walls more than five stories high. Hints that religious rituals took place in the sanctuary include such artifacts as ancient pieces of frankincense; and a large number of animal bones found on the site suggest that ritual sacrifice may have taken place there. Mausoleums, too, have been discovered nearby, by a team from the German Archaeological Institute, which promise to yield even more evidence.

As Glanzman explained to a reporter from *The Christian Science Monitor*, "Thousand of tons of wind-blown soil and lots of archaeological remains are there to uncover, so there are numerous discoveries to be made."

Will they find the Queen of Sheba at Mahram Bilqis? If they do, it will not be easy. "In order to know who she was," Glanzman told the *TIME* reporters, "we would need to find an inscription in Hebrew, and find it on an object that was unequivocally linked to the tenth century B.C. That's like trying to find a needle in a haystack that's been buried under 10 meters of sand."

7

The Many Faces of the Queen of Sheba

THE QUESTION "WHO DO YOU THINK YOU ARE, THE QUEEN OF SHEBA?" HAS been used (usually by women) to put women and girls "in their place" for many decades in the Western world. But just who the Queen of Sheba is still remains an open question. "Hollywood made Sheba a sex goddess, Solomon's lover, and they made her white," says Michael Wood in PBS's *Tales of Myths and Heroes*. "To Africans, though, she's black, and a woman of power. In Arabia she's half human, half demon . . . a woman who, as it says in one story, was not a woman, but a world."

Which brings this story full circle: Who *was* the Queen of Sheba?

One day, perhaps, the archaeologists who are currently working at the Mahram Bilqis site in Yemen—or somewhere else entirely—may discover her tomb, her name, records of her rule, an image of her face. For now, however, the Queen of Sheba remains what she has been throughout history: a woman of many faces that constantly change, depending on who's doing the looking.

INSIDER OR OUTSIDER?

In Africa and the Middle East, Makeda is the ultimate insider: revered as a monarch, admired for her intelligence and wisdom. Here, she is at home. Whether she is called Makeda, Bilqis or Balqis, or the Queen of Sheba, she's a well-known figure, even treated with affection ("like a great aunt," as Nicolas Clapp says) and seen as a real part of the history of nations. Oral history has kept her name current for centuries, and even today, people argue about the details of her life, keeping her tradition alive for new generations.

In the West, however, the Queen of Sheba has always been an outsider who "came from the ends of the earth." Although her story was told in the Old Testament, one of the foundational books of Judaism and Christianity, her name often carried the scent of scandal. Demonized early on, and dismissed as a biblical temptress, she has been seen as outside the cultural norms, outside polite society, sometimes even outside the human race. Still, her name continues to fascinate—it is used to sell everything from perfume to cat food. During the last centuries, the many movies about the romance of Solomon and Sheba have not done much to improve her image or impart real information. In North America, her tradition is not so well known. People have either heard of the Queen of Sheba, but do not know much about her; or they think of her as a scandalous figure. For many, she remains a mysterious stranger from another world.

THE FACE OF THE "OTHER"

"I am black and beautiful, O daughters of Jerusalem, like the tents of Kedar, like the curtains of Solomon." So speaks the

Queen of Sheba in the Song of Solomon (NRSV 1:5–6). With these words, she sets herself apart from the Western norm.

Coming from outside Solomon's culture—a worshipper of many gods entering a society that worshipped Yahweh above all others, speaking Sabean rather than Hebrew, and likely having a differently colored complexion—she was perceived as *different*, as *other*, right from the beginning. That difference soon took on a more physical and then supernatural dimension in tales and legends of the Middle East.

He built a glass floor to confirm the rumor that she had hairy legs, which Solomon (and perhaps the culture) considered unfeminine. As noted earlier, this disturbed him so much that he created a hair remover especially for her, adjusting her to the norms of his culture.

The problem with her foot went deeper. In Ethiopia, it was said to have resulted from an old injury. But legends that turned it into a foot that belonged to an animal—an ass's hoof, a goose's foot—seem designed to set her apart as not quite human. "This deformity," says Marina Warner in her essay "In and Out of the Fold," "captured the popular imagination and merged with Christian imagery of witches' distinguishing marks: the pagan queen, outside the fold, becomes lame in one foot, like the character in the children's game called Old Witch." In the Arabic tales, the Queen of Sheba's origins are more than hinted at: Here she is the child of a human father and mother who is a djinn.

The mystical Jewish Kabbalah, written in the late thirteenth century, implies that the queen was a witch. In the *Zohar,* "The Book of Splendor," one of the questions she asks Solomon (in Book III) concerns how to make a powerful "enchantment" that will protect against injury from weapons. Later, she is said to be a demon from the desert, and she is identified with the feared demon Lilith, who flew at night and seduced men.

And what of her belief in many gods? There, too, she was normalized. By the time she left Jerusalem, she approved of Solomon's God. In the Koran, she accepted Allah. Warner explains,

Artistic interpretations of Makeda, whose kingdoms were in Ethiopia and Yemen, were inaccurate, especially during the Renaissance period. Many paintings, such as *Two Riddles of the Queen of Sheba (above)*, contribute to the rumors and myths of the monarch's true image.

"Medieval Muslim folklore ... links heterodoxy [ideas that don't agree with accepted beliefs] with femaleness in the myth of Sheba. In these ... stories the queen is doubly a stranger to the center commanded by Solomon ... [who] acts as her savior, ... bringing her into the fold."

THE FACE ON THE BILLBOARD

Much of what Westerners know of the Queen of Sheba, beyond what they may read in the Bible, comes from what they see and read in the popular culture. Advertisers and enterprising marketers use the Queen of Sheba's allure—she is generally pictured as a Middle Eastern temptress—to beckon customers to all sorts of products. She is a cake (the French chocolate-almond Reine de Saba) and a cat food (Sheba) and a reason to buy perfume (Aqaba). All of this is nothing new: "Her . . . impact on the imagination of writers and artists down through the ages has been immense," writes art historian Alison Inglis in an article in *World of Antiques and Art.*

ART

In 2004, the Bowers Museum in Santa Ana, California, organized an exhibition of artifacts and cultural objects from the British Museum under the title "Queen of Sheba: Legend and Reality." Interestingly, many of the treasures from the Sabean civilization were from the first century, long after the dates for her rule. Other works on display included Renaissance art and even movie stills. Despite the fact that none of the artworks and artifacts could actually be linked to her directly, the fascinating aura that lingers over the Queen of Sheba was enough to generate a number of newspaper and magazine articles and interest in the exhibition.

For art historians familiar with works about her, this is nothing new. A piece from the Bowers show identified as "[a] parchment painted with the Ethiopian Sheba legend" tells the story in a series of comic-book-style images, a common technique in that country. A 1967 set of commemorative stamps from Yemen shows six different images, including *Solomon prostrating himself before a seated Bilqis.* A tinted drawing from Iran (1590–1600) depicts *The Queen of Sheba (Bilqis) Facing the Hoopoe, Solomon's Messenger.*

Warner says, "The blackness of the Queen of Sheba was taken for granted, naturally, by the Ethiopian Christians and their artists. Solomon, in the story scrolls and paintings, is ocher-colored, by contrast. . . . Sometimes, she says, there's a kind of feeling that European artists are skirting the issue." Most Western artists, until the nineteenth century, drew, sculpted, and painted the Queen of Sheba as a European.

Her image appeared in art dating at least back to the Middle Ages, when illuminated manuscripts show *Solomon receiving Sheba, who is bringing gifts* and *The Queen of Sheba Before Solomon, testing him with questions*, among other biblical scenes. She was also a popular subject during the Renaissance and afterward. Piero della Francesca painted her in the fifteenth century, Raphael painted her in the early sixteenth century, and Peter Paul Rubens painted her in the early seventeenth century, to name only a few.

In some of these earlier artworks, only the presence of camels, or an African servant, gave any hint at all of her origins. This changed in the late nineteenth century, says Inglis, when "a new interest in historicism focused attention on 'authentic' costumes, racial types and architectural settings." By then,

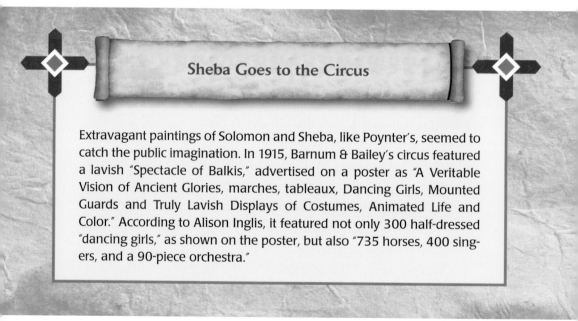

Sheba Goes to the Circus

Extravagant paintings of Solomon and Sheba, like Poynter's, seemed to catch the public imagination. In 1915, Barnum & Bailey's circus featured a lavish "Spectacle of Balkis," advertised on a poster as "A Veritable Vision of Ancient Glories, marches, tableaux, Dancing Girls, Mounted Guards and Truly Lavish Displays of Costumes, Animated Life and Color." According to Alison Inglis, it featured not only 300 half-dressed "dancing girls," as shown on the poster, but also "735 horses, 400 singers, and a 90-piece orchestra."

people were becoming more familiar with how the ancient Middle East might have looked, and Sir Edward Poynter's *The Visit of the Queen of Sheba to King Solomon* (1890) is famous for its use of detail and its more authentic portrayal of Solomon and Sheba.

LITERATURE AND MUSIC

Books and poetry, too, have been inspired by the Queen of Sheba since at least the fourteenth century, when Italian author Giovanni Boccaccio wrote about her (as Nicaula) in his *De mulieribus claris,* "Concerning Famous Women," with a great deal of admiration:

> As far as I can determine, Nicaula was a product of remote and barbaric Ethiopia. She is the more worthy of remembrance as her splendid moral principles had their origin among uncivilized folk.
>
> The following facts are known (if we can believe the ancient sources): When the dynasty of the Pharaohs came to an end, Nicaula, either as a descendant of this or another line, was a famous queen of Ethiopia and Egypt; some authorities say that she was also the queen of Arabia; she had a royal palace on Meroe, a very large island in the Nile, and her massive wealth was thought to surpass that of every mortal.
>
> Despite the pleasures that riches can bring, we read that Nicaula did not abandon herself to idleness or feminine luxury. Quite the contrary: though her teacher remains anonymous, we do know that she was wonderfully learned in the natural sciences. Sacred Scripture, which authoritatively indicates Nicaula's existence, also seems to attest to this. . . .
>
> Nicaula . . . abandoned her own illustrious kingdom, setting out from Meroe, which is situated practically on the other side of the world, and came to Jerusalem to hear him. She crossed Ethiopia, Egypt, the coast of the Red Sea, and

the deserts of Arabia with such a splendid entourage, glorious pomp, and multitude of royal retainers that Solomon himself, the wealthiest of all kings, was astonished by her magnificence.

In 1919, Irish poet William Butler Yeats wrote the poem "Solomon to Sheba," in which they profess their love and equal intelligence:

> There's not a man or woman
> Born under the skies
> Dare match in learning with us two.

Rudyard Kipling wrote about "Balkis, the Most Beautiful," in one of his *Just So Stories,* "The Butterfly That Stamped." In this story, Balkis—one of his "nine hundred and ninety-nine" is "nearly as wise as he"—although, in the end, she proves just a bit wiser, and "[t]hen they went up to the Palace and lived happily ever afterwards."

Thomas B. Aldrich's book *The Queen of Sheba,* written in 1876, was just one of many books of fiction and nonfiction to use the queen's name to tell a story. In the nineteenth century, she was written about more than once in compendiums of "women in the Bible." Her story is still the basis for literature in the twenty-first century, undergoing yet another evolution in the process. In India Edgehill's 2004 historical novel *Wisdom's Daughter,* the queen—called by one reviewer "equal rights Sheba"—seeks out King Solomon to help her find a female heir to replace her on the throne. The 1999 historical romance by Janice L. Dennie, *Moon Goddess: The Queen of Sheba,* Princess Makeda of Sheba, seeking a political alliance, cannot help falling in love with Solomon, the King of Judah.

The romance of Solomon and Sheba lent itself to spectacle, and the story was a popular one for opera. In 1749, composer George Frideric Handel wrote this oratorio in his opera *Solomon:*

> *But to hear fair truth distilling*
> *In expression choice and thrilling*
> *From that tongue so soft and killing*
> *That my soul does most delight . . .*
> *And now, illustrious prince, receive*
> *Such tribute as my realm can give.*

In 1862, the French composer Charles Gounod composed *La Reine de Saba (The Queen of Sheba).* The opera *Die Konigin von Saba (The Queen of Sheba)* entertained popular audiences in 1875.

In the twentieth-century Broadway musical *My Fair Lady,* Professor Henry Higgins informs the unschooled Cockney girl Eliza Doolittle, "Why, I could pass you off as the queen of Sheba!" The Queen of Sheba's name is still turning up in the lyrics of popular songs. As Bonnie Raitt sings in John Hiatt's song "A Thing Called Love": "You know I ain't no Queen of Sheba."

THE FACE OF A "LOVE GODDESS"

The mundane political tale of an international trade agreement did not catch the popular imagination. But—as the number of operas based on the subject demonstrate—the idea of a sizzling romance between two attractive and intelligent monarchs caught on early and continues to this day.

The romance of Solomon and Sheba seems made for movies, and as the twentieth century began, filmmakers discovered it almost immediately. In 1921, the fledgling Fox Studio filmed a hit movie (unfortunately lost) complete with dancing girls called *The Queen of Sheba,* advertised as "The Love Romance of the World's Most Beautiful Woman." In 1959, Yul Brynner played Solomon, and Gina Lollobrigida played an "Italian bombshell"

The tale of Solomon and Makeda's relationship was the perfect storyline for the big screen. Several movies were made depicting their love affair, all touting the Queen of Sheba as one of the most beautiful women of the world. In 1921's *The Queen of Sheba*, actress Betty Blythe *(above)*, known for acting in exotic films, was costumed in revealing outfits but portrayed the queen as dignified and strong.

version of Sheba in the Technicolor spectacular *Solomon and Sheba*—"Behold! The love story of the ages!" declares the movie's poster. It was not until 1995, in the TV movie *Solomon and*

Sheba, starring Halle Berry, that the queen was finally portrayed as a woman of color.

AS FEMINIST ICON

In Jacki Lyden's 1997 memoir *Daughter of the Queen of Sheba,* her mother's descent into mental illness is announced with these words:

> "I am the Queen of Sheba," my mother announced to me in a regal voice. She had taken the silky yellow sheets from her voluptuous bed and twisted them around her torso like a toga. . . . She'd used eye pencil on her arms, and drawn hieroglyphics. . . . Her long auburn hair was swept up and crowned with an old tiara that we girls had played with as children.

Does a woman have to be mentally ill to identify with the Queen of Sheba? In the West, her name has been used with scorn for a long time. When many Americans think about the Queen of Sheba, the images of centuries of popular culture—the folktales and the paintings, the circus acts and movie vamps—combine to conjure nothing more than a beautiful pagan woman who thought she was smarter than Solomon, hung around his palace, used her sexuality to get what she wanted, and then abruptly went home. In these portrayals, her very best qualities—strength, intelligence, beauty, leadership—are used against her. Why? As Warner says, although the Bible talks at length about her wealth, "it's her mind the writers invite us to admire . . . Solomon, the wisest man on earth, trusts Sheba with all he knows and understands." The Queen of Sheba's most recent face is that of a feminist icon. In 1980, for example, the United Kingdom collective Sheba Feminist Press came out of the British women's movement. As Fontaine told *The Christian Science Monitor,* "We've taught [ourselves] that women belong in a domestic sphere, but here's a woman who succeeded in such a powerful way that three major world religions remember her."

A clear image of Makeda is once again emerging, an image that owes much to the *Kebra Nagast.* Wendy Belcher, in her article "Medieval African and European Texts About the Queen of Sheba" in the May 2006 *Newsletter of the UCLA Center for the Study of Women,* says, "In stark contrast [to the medieval Arabic and Jewish Sheba traditions], the African Christian tradition centers on an African woman, one who is beautiful, wise, virtuous, wealthy, and powerful. . . . She is not demonic but pure, not naïve but wise, not subordinate but free."

Not subordinate, but free. A strong female ruler, Makeda was one of very few such women in a world ruled largely by men, and where kings had many concubines and many wives and were not used to dealing with women political leaders. Her intelligence—along with her determination to use it to further the fortunes of her country—set her apart and made her impossible to dismiss.

8

The Legacy of the Queen of Sheba

FROM THE TENTH CENTURY B.C. TO THE TWENTY-FIRST CENTURY, THE STORY of the Queen of Sheba has evolved, accumulating its many cultural and societal transformations and growing stronger, more colorful, and more compelling with each passing year. Yes, her "real story" has yet to be told in full, awaiting the evidence to be provided by archaeologists and scholars; and no one can yet point to her tomb and say, "There lies the Queen of Sheba!" Yet it is almost impossible to believe that someday her tomb will be discovered, the records of her reign pored over in universities and museums. This extraordinary woman, who lived so many thousands of years ago, seems even more alive today. And, seen in the light of the twenty-first century, she seems even more remarkable.

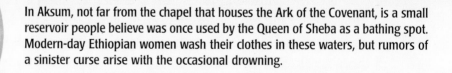

In Aksum, not far from the chapel that houses the Ark of the Covenant, is a small reservoir people believe was once used by the Queen of Sheba as a bathing spot. Modern-day Ethiopian women wash their clothes in these waters, but rumors of a sinister curse arise with the occasional drowning.

Makeda was a daring and outstanding leader of a kingdom that united two unrelated cultures, Ethiopia and South Arabia, and made them one. Under her rule, two different lands, both bursting with resources valued by the entire ancient world, were able to find new markets for those commodities and safe passage for their merchants. She was a visionary at the beginning of a golden age, and what she envisioned for Saba came to pass.

Makeda was beautiful, and history has not let anyone forget just how beautiful she was. But she did not use her great beauty to manipulate. Instead, she used her intelligence to cut through preconceptions and to persuade, and she was respected and remembered for it. Unwilling to accept what she was told without question, she was more than willing to risk her life on the belief that she could tell truth from fiction, that she could devise a bold plan and make it work. Her actions truly speak louder than words.

Makeda was an astute politician. Her fertile mind created questions that impressed Solomon, the wisest king in the world, with her wisdom. Together, the two wise monarchs formed an alliance beneficial for both cultures, not only in terms of politics and products, but in terms of philosophy. Together, the priestess of nature gods and the worshipper of one supreme God respected each others' beliefs. Makeda returned to her people with a new vision of how the world might be.

For Ethiopia, Makeda also brought back a son, a living symbol of the unification of the two cultures and part of a guiding historical narrative. Today, her spirit, story, and memory continue to be a powerful inspiration not only for Ethiopians and Rastafarians but for many people of color throughout the world.

Today, when strong, intelligent women are respected rather than feared, and are leading not only nations but corporations and social movements of many kinds, Makeda, the Queen of Sheba, is finding a new place of honor in the West as a feminist

Above, a Yemeni scholar carefully examines a funeral marker used to build a pillar at the Sanctuary of Bilqis. Discovered outside the town of Marib, the sanctuary is believed to be the Queen of Sheba's personal temple, and may reveal concrete evidence of her existence.

icon and role model. No longer marginalized as a siren, a tramp, a witch, or a demon, she is what she always was: a beautiful, wise woman and a bold and forward-thinking political leader. Seen in the clear light of historical understanding, the Queen of Sheba stands as an example for all women who want to leave home to explore the world, ask intelligent questions of it, and return home with more than they could ever imagine.

CHRONOLOGY

1500 B.C.	Irrigation of croplands becomes possible in South Arabia when a dam is built to block flooding in the Wadi Adana, near Marib
1400 B.C.	The Epigraphic South Arabic (ESA) alphabet and script is developed
1300 B.C.	The camel is domesticated in South Arabia
1200 B.C.	Formal rule of Saba begins, along with an early merchant state
1100 B.C.	The camel saddle is invented, making long-distance trading possible
ca. 1004 B.C.	King David captures Jerusalem from the Jebusites and makes Jerusalem the capital of Israel
1000 B.C.	Sabean caravans begin the long-distance trade in incense
ca. 980–950 B.C.	The earliest and latest possible dates for reign of King Solomon of Israel
ca. 970–940 B.C.	The earliest and latest possible dates for the Queen of Sheba's reign
ca. 955–945 B.C.	The Queen of Sheba goes to Jerusalem

GLOSSARY

◆ ◆ ◆

Aksum   The Queen of Sheba's capital in Ethiopia.

Almakah   The Sabean Moon god; also Almaqah, Ilumquh.

Bilqis   The Middle Eastern name for the Queen of Sheba; also Balqis, Balkis.

ESA   Epigraphic South Arabic, the written language of the Sabeans.

Kebra Nagast   "The Glory of Kings," the sacred text of Ethiopian Christians and Jamaican Rastafarians, which tells the story of Queen Makeda. It is believed to have been compiled in the fourteenth century.

Koran   The sacred text of Islam; it includes stories of the Queen of Sheba.

Mahram Bilqis   "The Temple of Bilqis," or "the Queen of Sheba's Sanctified Place," near the old city of Marib in Yemen, is said to have been a Sabean temple of the Moon god Almakah, and the earliest known Arabian temple. It has been continuously excavated by an international team of archaeologists since 1988.

Makeda   "Greatness"; the Ethiopian name for the Queen of Sheba.

Marib   The Queen of Sheba's South Arabian capital; also called Kitor.

Menelik I   The son of Queen Makeda and King Solomon, and the first king of the Solomonic Dynasty.

Polytheism   Religion in which more than one god is worshipped; the Sabeans were polytheists.

Saba   The Queen of Sheba's kingdom, which comprised parts of South Arabia (now present-day Yemen) and Ethiopia.

Sirwah   Thought to be the capital of Saba before Marib.

Solomonic monarchy   Ethiopia's hereditary dynasty, begun in the tenth century B.C. by Menelik I, son of Queen Makeda and King Solomon, and ending in 1974 with Emperor Haile Selassie.

Yahweh   A name of God used by the Jews in Solomon's time.

BIBLIOGRAPHY

◆ ◆ ◆

Achtemeir, Paul J., gen. ed. *Harper's Bible Dictionary, 1985*. San Francisco: Harper & Row Publishers, 1985.

Budge, E. A. Wallis. *The Queen of Sheba and Her Only Son Menyelek. [Kebra Negast]* London: Oxford University Press, 1932.

Clapp, Nicholas. *Sheba: Through the Desert in Search of the Legendary Queen*. Boston: Houghton Mifflin, 2001.

Ginzburg, Louis. *The Legends of the Jews*. Philadelphia: Jewish Publication Society of America, 1987.

Lemonick, Michael D., and Andrea Dorfman. "Searching for Sheba." *TIME* magazine. September 10, 2001,

Warner, Maria. *From the Beast to the Blonde: On Fairy Tales and Their Tellers*. New York: Farrar, Straus and Giroux, 1994.

———. "In and out of the Fold: Wisdom, Danger, and Glamour in the Tale of the Queen of Sheba." In C. Buchmann and C. Spiegel. *Out of the Garden: Women Writers on the Bible*. New York: Fawcett Columbine, 1994.

WEB SITES

Arnold, Catherine. "Mystery of an African Queen." *Guardian Unlimited/Travel,* July 3, 2006, Available online at http://travel.guardian.couk/article/2006/jul/03/Ethiopia.yemen.

Boustany, Nora. "Putting the Queen of Sheba to the Test." *The Washington Post,* September 5, 2003, Available online at http://www.washingtonpost.com.

Goodale, Gloria. "Treasure Fit for a Queen." *The Christian Science Monitor,* November 12, 2004, Available online at http://www.csmonitor.com/2004/1112/p12s03-alar.html.

Rynor, Michah. "Scholars Search for the Queen of Sheba." University of Toronto. *News@Uof T,* May 18, 2005, Available online at http://www.news.utoronto.ca/bin6/050518–1387.asp.

Steiner, Margaret. "Jerusalem in the 10th/9th Centuries B.C." The Bible and Interpretation. August 2004. Available online at http://www.bibleinterp.com/articles/Steiner-10th-9th_Century_1.htm.

University of Calgary. "Arabian Desert Surrenders Queen of Sheba's Secrets." September 12, 2000, Available online at http://www.ucalgary.ca/UofC/events/unicomm/NewsReleases/queen.htm.

FURTHER READING

◆ ◆ ◆

Clapp, Nicholas. *Sheba: Through the Desert in Search of the Legendary Queen.* Boston: Houghton Mifflin, 2001.

Hausman, Gerald, and Ziggy Marley. *Kebra Negast: A Book of Rastafarian Wisdom.* New York: St. Martin's Press, 1967.

Simpson, John, ed. *The Queen of Sheba: Treasures from Ancient Yemen.* London: British Museum Press, 2002.

Warner, Maria. *From the Beast to the Blonde: On Fairy Tales and Their Tellers.* New York: Farrar, Straus and Giroux, 1994.

WEB SITES

American Foundation for the Study of Man
www.afsm.org

Caravan Kingdoms: Yemen and the Ancient Incense Trade
www.asia.si.edu

Jewish Encyclopedia
www.jewishencyclopedia.com

Metropolitan Museum of Art Timeline of Art History: Foundations of Aksumite Civilization and Its Christian Legacy (first to seventh centuries A.D.)
www.metmuseum.org/toah/hd/aksu/hd_aksu_1.htm

Queen of Sheba: Legend and Reality. Treasures from the British Museum
www.bowers.org/Sheba/Sheba.html

Queen of Sheba: Treasures from Ancient Yemen
www.thebritishmuseum.ac.uk/compass

The Connection: The Queen of Sheba (May 21, 2001)
http://www.theconnection.org/shows/2001/05/20010521_b_main.asp

PHOTO CREDITS

◆ ◆ ◆

INDEX

ABOUT THE AUTHORS

◆ ◆ ◆

NAOMI LUCKS has worked as a writer, editor, and author coach for more than two decades. She has edited and developed topics for book projects, ranging from art to health to professional mediation. Lucks has also written Web sites, edited a magazine about horses, and traveled to Peru and China on writing assignments.

ARTHUR SCHLESINGER, JR. is remembered as the leading American historian of our time. He won the Pulitzer Prize for his books *The Age of Jackson* (1945) and *A Thousand Days* (1965), which also won the National Book Award. Schlesinger was the Albert Schweitzer Professor of the Humanities at the City University of New York and was involved in several other Chelsea House projects, including the series *Revolutionary War Leaders*, *Colonial Leaders*, and *Your Government*.